Teaching Inclusively in
Higher Education

Teaching Inclusively in Higher Education

Moira A. Fallon

College at Brockport
State University of New York

Susan C. Brown

University of Central Florida
(Retired)

INFORMATION AGE PUBLISHING, INC.
Charlotte, NC • www.infoagepub.com

Library of Congress Cataloging-in-Publication Data

Teaching inclusively in higher education / Moira A. Fallon, Susan C. Brown, [editors].
   p. cm.
  Includes bibliographical references.
  ISBN 978-1-60752-445-8 (pbk.) – ISBN 978-1-60752-446-5 (hardcover) – ISBN 978-1-60752-447-2 (e-book)
1. Education, Higher–Philosophy. 2. Inclusive education–Philosophy. I. Brown, Susan C. II. Fallon, Moira A.
  LB2322.2.T424 2010
  378.1'25–dc22

2010000952

Printed in the United States of America

CONTENTS

Preface vii

PART I

STUDENTS AS DIVERSE INDIVIDUALS AND MEMBERS OF INCLUSIVE GROUPS

1. A Student-Centered Approach to College Classrooms 3
    Moira A. Fallon and Susan C. Brown

2. Students as Cultural Beings 17
    Susan C. Brown

3. When Reading in College is a Problem:
    What Really Matters? 39
    Alexander B. Casareno

PART II

INCLUSIVE INSTRUCTORS AS STRATEGIC LEADERS AND CO-LEARNERS

4. Changing Instructional Strategies and Methods to Meet the
    Needs of All Learners 61
    Moira A. Fallon

5. The Changing Role of Instructors as
    Both Leaders and Learners 77
    Paul T. Parkison

6. Using Language Successfully in the College Classroom.............. 95
    Ellyn L. Arwood and Joanna R. Kaakinen

PART III

TECHNOLOGICAL CLASSROOM CLIMATES AS INCLUSIVE LEARNING COMMUNITIES

7. Technology Connecting Curriculum, Instruction, and
    Assessment 115
    Mark C. Geary

8. Reaching Students through a Virtual Community 135
    Shelley B. Harris, Jennifer C. Wilson, and Jacqueline M. Ferguson

9. The Technological Age of Teaching 155
    Michelle Pulaski Behling and Beth Gordon Klingner

10. Applications to Inclusive College Classrooms............................171
    Moira A. Fallon, Susan C. Brown, and Alexander B. Casareno

    Authors' Biographies: In the Order They Appear in the Book....185

PREFACE

The purpose of this book is to assist all college instructors in higher education to better meet the changing and diverse needs of their student populations. More than ever before, college students come from diverse cultural and experiential backgrounds. They have diverse academic and personal needs that may, at times, conflict in priority. Higher education today is rapidly changing and college instructors are being presented with new types of students. These students often have clear goals for improving their lives, but at the same time lack what might have been considered to be basic skills necessary for success in a college or university setting. College today is becoming a right for all, rather than a privilege for a few.

The changing face of students in institutions of higher education today is causing a shift in college classrooms. Student diversity impacts a variety of learning outcomes, including that of teaching methods, the learning process itself, the pace of learning, technological tools, use of text and print, and the framework for reading, among others. This diversity of students can be a tremendous asset in that students bring more to the college classroom in terms of experiences and life. More college students are active in our globalized society and may be more understanding of other cultures than students of past decades.

The rich diversity of students may also impact college instructors' assumptions that all students bring the same skill sets to college classrooms, particularly in terms of reading or language ability. For example, the traditional assignment of reading 50 pages of text per night may not be pos-

Teaching Inclusively in Higher Education, pages vii–xi
Copyright © 2010 by Information Age Publishing
All rights of reproduction in any form reserved.

sible for some students. Yet, all college students have experiences and potential that, appropriately mined by inclusive instructors, can add richness to course content in a variety of ways such as class discussions or research projects. New ways of working with students can help in developing student potential. The embedded use of technology, for instance, can be a great equalizer among students who may vary tremendously in their written or oral expression skills.

Inclusive college instructors today must reach and bring all students into the college or university setting in an inclusive manner. Inclusive teaching means to teach in a manner so all students can process and understand the material in whatever ways are best for them. Inclusive education is a core belief with a flexible set of teaching practices that supports all students' learning. College instructors must understand the full range of student diversity. Instructors must also recognize that previous ways of teaching will not be effective with this new generation of college students.

This book will provide valuable instructional strategies and practical techniques for instructors to develop inclusive college classrooms that promote the learning of all students. The emphasis of this book is on college student-focused strategies for teaching inclusively. The practical nature of this book addresses the major issue of higher education teaching today: the need to reach all higher education students using active learning strategies. Ensuring greater student success and higher achievement among college students can only add quality to the professional workforce.

As centers for excellence in learning and teaching are established in colleges and universities, the scholarship of teaching is developing as a vital part of skills for college instructors. This book is meant to be used as a practical means of conveying the scholarship of teaching into inclusive teaching strategies for all college instructors, regardless of discipline or content. Each chapter makes explicit the theoretical research basis of the chapter content, presents instructional and methodological strategies, and shares resources or templates for inclusive instructional use. Each chapter also contains specific inclusive strategies that can be translated into any content area or adapted to meet any individual needs of instructors. The final chapter in the book contains application scenarios that demonstrate the instructional choices inclusive instructors may make in their college classroom settings. It is hoped that these scenarios will help inclusive college instructors to become more creative and utilize research-based, instructional techniques for their college students.

The book is particularly valuable for all college instructors without a background in the discipline of education, even though the authors and editors are from the field of education, as well as many of the instructional methods. The book has the potential of being a guidebook on active learning strategies for tenure-track and adjunct instructors at all levels and disciplines in institutions of higher education. With the increased interest in the quality of college-level teaching and the corresponding emphasis on professional development in teaching, this book could be used in teaching and learning centers in community colleges and universities. It could also be used by individual instructors who wish to update or refine their instruction. The methods shared here have been tried and refined with a wide variety of students and in many differing college classrooms across the United States.

The chapters in this book follow the same sequence. Each chapter starts with key terms, which are later defined in the chapter. Next are reflective questions which can be used to guide reading or for group discussion. The body of the chapter contains the theoretical basis followed by suggestions for implementation of the chapter content. Also included in each chapter are practical examples and instructor resources for use by college instructors in any discipline.

The book is divided into three major sections, each section addressing a particular area of student need that college instructors should address. The first section describes the increasing diversity of students in college classrooms today. In many, if not most cases, students are different in a variety of cultural ways from one another and from their instructors. These students are active learners with unique backgrounds and skills. They have multilayered lives with increasing demands and responsibilities and they move at a hectic pace. They juggle competing interests, the least of which might be their college course demands. Often, they are more technologically savvy than their instructors in the use of multimedia and communication tools.

The chapter authors in the first section of the book focus on the wide diversity of the students and discuss the differences among college instructors and their students. Many instructors today are older and less comfortable with the technology that their students use. Popular cultural interests often vary widely between instructors and students, with significant differences in music, film, television, and extracurricular activities. There are fewer areas of common interests to share or to integrate into the classroom setting. Workloads among college instructors today are significantly heavier than they have ever been in the past. This leaves less time to interact with students and to get to know their individual needs.

The second section of the book is focused on how inclusive instructors can reach and teach all of their students. Given these intrinsic differences between college students and their instructors, mismatches can often occur. These mismatches are significant in that they impede instruction and the real learning that should take place in the college classroom setting. The instructional methods chosen by college instructors have a direct impact on their students' processes of learning. How should instructors change their own teaching methods and technological tools in response to the changing faces and minds of these college students? Inclusive instructional strategies and devices must be designed to as to motivate and engage these learners in new ways.

The chapter authors in the second section of the book explore the inclusive instructional strategies, including technological tools that the instructor should master. New techniques in brain-based learning, visual processing, and language learning and development can assist students in better mastery of the content. The choices made by college instructors in the use of instructional methods create inclusive learning environments in which students can respond and learn. Of critical importance is the alignment of curriculum, instruction, and assessment. Regardless of the discipline, the content must be taught so that all students have the opportunity to understand the information and are given the chance to demonstrate their knowledge and skills. Using these instructional strategies, the instructor role seems to shift, from that of a director or controller of the intake of learning to that of a facilitator or provider of learning opportunities. This shift in role for the instructors can better mesh with the salient characteristics of diverse learners and improve the quality of the learning process for all.

The third section of the book is on developing the technological classroom climate as an inclusive learning community. Of equal importance to the previous sections about the roles of the students and instructors is the development of the third element: the technological classroom climate. Both instructors and the students often assume that this is not important, but difficulties in this area can lead to the difference between mediocre results and superior ones. The interconnectedness of curriculum, instruction, and assessment is explored within today's technological world. A safe and secure online world is essential to any discipline and content area. College instructors can help their students to be successful with technology, as well as help create a more inclusive learning community.

The authors of the first three chapters in the third section explain the importance of developing an inclusive learning community with the help of technology. Often college instructors are facilitators of the environment, working within pre-determined restraints in the physical and psychological structure of the classroom and the quality of the available technology. The students, on the other hand, are the consumers of the space and have an active role to be empowered to use it in their learning process. They have varying technological tools available to them that they may not have applied to the content area. This creates a tension or balance optimizing teaching and learning. Using many forms of media can help students to think more critically and to apply their learning more deeply within their given field or profession.

The final chapter of the third section differs from all the previous chapters in that it focuses on applying some of the many suggestions and strategies found throughout the book. The authors of this chapter present four different classroom scenarios, showing typical situations and student populations that college instructors might face. The scenarios demonstrate the thinking and planning processes of instructors at the beginning, the middle, and the end of their courses as they try to teach more inclusively. The modifications suggested in the scenarios are by no means the only ones that could have been chosen but they demonstrate possibilities for effective changes for developing inclusive classrooms.

A book of this practical nature is unique in today's market. This book is meant to be a guide for college instructors working with diverse student populations. It fills a gap in the market that other books have missed or only partially filled. With the increased interest in college-level teaching and the corresponding emphasis on professional development in teaching, this book could be used in teaching and learning centers in community colleges and universities as well as used by individual instructors. The focus on diverse college students in institutions of higher education is unique. The emphasis on creating inclusive learning environments is a major priority. The book contains the basic theoretical background for the instructional methods and provides practical strategies and techniques for classroom application. The book is applicable to any college academic content or discipline. The authors explore the inclusive instructional strategies that are basically required to reach and teach these students, including technological tools that all college instructors should master.

PART I

STUDENTS AS DIVERSE INDIVIDUALS AND MEMBERS OF INCLUSIVE GROUPS

CHAPTER 1

A STUDENT-CENTERED APPROACH TO COLLEGE CLASSROOMS

Moira A. Fallon and Susan C. Brown

KEY TERMS

Culture; Cultural Mismatches; Discrimination; Inclusion or Inclusive Education; Learning Styles; Multiple Intelligences

REFLECTIVE QUESTIONS

- How are professional and personal interactions at the heart of being culturally competent and being inclusive?
- Why is it important for instructors to meet the needs of all their learners or are some students simply not meant for college?
- What aspects of curriculum, instruction, and assessment should college instructors consider in order to provide for all students?

Teaching Inclusively in Higher Education, pages 3–16
Copyright © 2010 by Information Age Publishing
3

INTRODUCTION

Today's college classrooms are inherently different places than they were in the past. Going to college has become a right and a necessity rather than a privilege for a large part of the American population. For many students, going to college is seen as a way of bettering themselves and thus bettering the outcomes for their families. More and more students are showing up on college campuses with a strong desire to get a college diploma, but they have fewer skills for being successful in the college setting than previous generations of students. Most college students have spent previous academic years learning how to succeed individually, how to stand out, and how to be a star. They have also learned that conforming and not challenging authority are ways to get ahead. Yet students in the 21st century must be global thinkers who readily work in teams and use creativity in their problem solving.

Today's college classrooms are also different from past ones because they contain many more students with special needs. The practice of *inclusion* or *inclusive education* has had a significant impact on college classrooms. This practice is more than the old concept of mainstreaming, the practice of educating students with special needs in regular education Kindergarten to Grade 12 (K–12) classrooms for select periods of time based on skill level. In the mainstreaming model, the majority of the education of students with special needs takes place in a special education classroom. Inclusion, by contrast, "is a model that begins with the right of every child to be in the mainstream of education" (Sapon-Shevin, 2007, p. 6). The fundamental principle of inclusive education is, according to Kunc (1992), the "valuing of diversity within the human community" (p. 38). It is a philosophy and set of teaching practices that support the belief that all students should be full and permanent members of the classroom community regardless of differences related to (dis)ability, race, language, religion, and class. Students and their families who are used to having their needs met in the general education classroom setting want that practice to continue in the college setting. As a result of inclusive practices in K–12 classrooms, students who would not have been accepted by colleges and universities in the past are now being encouraged to continue their education. Yet to succeed, many of these students need more individualized approaches to learning. Supported by federal and state laws, inclusive practices have become a part of student rights in college classrooms.

Today's college classrooms are also places where a wide variety of technological tools are being used and where students are expected to be technologically competent. Many students come to the classrooms well versed in several forms of technology, including PDAs, cell phones operating a multitude of tasks, and multi-media such as DVDs and Blu-Ray. Yet they often do not know how to apply their technological skills to academic learning. For students with special needs, technology is even more critical. Students with disabilities in the college setting have the right to access technology that compensates for their disability. Assistive technology (AT) is designed specifically to compensate for a disability and can empower students to accomplish a variety of academic tasks. The effective use of technological devices concerns both students and instructors.

As the classroom student population has continued to diversify and as knowledge about teaching and learning has continued to expand, the role of college instructors has evolved from that of the traditional sage on the stage to the more challenging but more effective one of a guide on the side. Instructors face a good deal of pressure to keep up with this evolving 21st-century higher education scene. An essential first step for instructors in the transformative process is to focus on including all students and incorporating the diversity they bring into college classrooms.

STUDENTS AS DIVERSE LEARNERS

Today's university students in the United States are more culturally diverse than ever before. *Culture* in this book is seen in the broad sense as "the values, traditions, social and political relationships, and worldview created, shared, and transformed by a group of people" (Nieto, 2000, p. 138). Important cultural differences in the college classroom may be any combination of age, race/ethnicity, social class, sex, language, religion, sexual orientation, ableness (special needs), regionality, and nationality (Brown & Kysilka, 2002). Culture involves beliefs, values, assumptions, and attitudes and determines individual and group world views. Cultural influences and individual preferences influence the ways students think, learn, act, and react in classroom settings.

Statistics indicate that the average age of undergraduate and graduate students is older, with several students in their 30s, 40s, and even 50s in classes. The students come from a broader range of racial and class backgrounds. Most if not all students have a greater familiarity with technology than ever before. Many come to college with technological skills that exceed those of their instructors. Overall, women outnumber men in undergraduate courses, but decades-old gender patterns for majors continue. Students from working class or poor families and students who have English as a second language are much more common in university classrooms. Students also have a wider variety of religious backgrounds, from Christian fundamentalists to Muslims to Buddhists. Although gay students have always been a part of the university student population, gays, lesbians, bisexuals, and transsexuals are more likely to be out than ever before. Students with special needs are more common on campus, thanks in part to legislation and advocacy groups. Finally, university students come from a wide variety of geographical areas in the world. Although state universities tend to have a majority of students from their respective states, out-of-state and international students have also increased in numbers, especially in graduate courses.

This richness of various cultural groups adds tremendously to the educational experiences of all, instructors and students alike. Yet this richness also poses a huge challenge to instructors who are increasingly discovering that the old ways of teaching and learning do not work well for all students in the diverse university population. In the past, students who struggled academically were too often considered poor students and were expected or even encouraged to leave. Today, with increasing competition for students, retention rates are closely analyzed and programs implemented to minimize student drop-outs. Instructors are encouraged by administration to play a supportive role and are expected to spend out-of-class time tutoring and counseling individual students. Today's students also know their rights and demand that instructors pay attention to their specific needs. They feel entitled to a college education, not privileged to be one of the few chosen for higher education as in former times. They see themselves as consumers and demand services and products for their money, although they are not always wisely or well informed.

CULTURAL INFLUENCES AND DISCRIMINATION

As mentioned earlier, cultural influences can include any one or combination of age, race/ethnicity, gender, class, language religion, sexual orientation, ableness, regionality, and nationality (Brown & Kysilka, 2002). As humans we are bound to others by many obvious and not-so-obvious ties because of our cultural and personal backgrounds. Surface cultural influences such as special foods and dances are easier for individuals to recognize and appreciate. Deep cultural influences such as gender roles and extended family commitments are harder to accept in others and to change in oneself. Like an iceberg, surface culture is only a small part of the whole (see Figure 1.1). The deep culture below the surface involves core beliefs and values. Assumptions, attitudes, and ultimately behavior usually come from deep cultural influences.

Cultural influences are also what sometimes separate people, either as individuals or as part of a specific cultural group. Depending on different situations, any one or any combination of cultural influences can affect behaviors. In the United States, the three cultural groupings that have traditionally been the most volatile are race, social class, and gender. Now, with

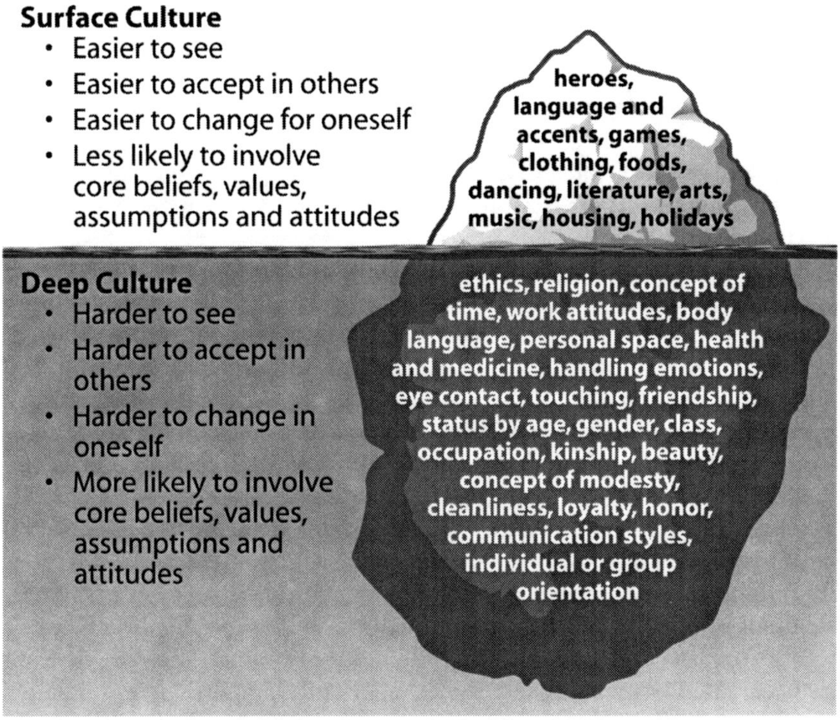

Surface Culture
- Easier to see
- Easier to accept in others
- Easier to change for oneself
- Less likely to involve core beliefs, values, assumptions and attitudes

heroes, language and accents, games, clothing, foods, dancing, literature, arts, music, housing, holidays

Deep Culture
- Harder to see
- Harder to accept in others
- Harder to change in oneself
- More likely to involve core beliefs, values, assumptions and attitudes

ethics, religion, concept of time, work attitudes, body language, personal space, health and medicine, handling emotions, eye contact, touching, friendship, status by age, gender, class, occupation, kinship, beauty, concept of modesty, cleanliness, loyalty, honor, communication styles, individual or group orientation

FIGURE 1.1. Adapted from Brown & Kysilka, 2002, p. 69.

the U.S. events on September 11, 2001 (9/11), and the war on terrorism, religion has also triggered serious cultural clashes.

When cultural differences occur, cultural conflicts are likely to follow. If those individuals or groups involved have equal status or power, then negotiations can be on a give-and-take basis with both sides influencing the outcome. *Discrimination* is a result of uneven power dynamics and occurs when the more powerful individual or group uses that power to act against the other. Koppelman and Goodhart (2008) discuss three types of discrimination: individual, cultural, and institutional. They see individual discrimination such as sexism as involving prejudiced attitudes and actions against individuals or groups based on that specific characteristic (sex). Date rape and domestic abuse are extreme but all too common examples. Cultural discrimination, according to Koppelman and Goodhart, involves prejudices and actions embedded in the culture of the dominant group and practiced over time. For instance, historically in the U.S., women were viewed as the weaker sex and as emotionally rather than rationally driven so were denied the vote until 1920. Finally, institutional discrimination, as described by Koppelman and Goodhart (2008), involves the privilege and advantage found in institutional policies and practices for specific groups. Legal legislation in Europe and the U.S. for centuries forced women to give their property and money to their husbands upon marriage—still a common practice in some countries. All three forms of discrimination can be readily found in American colleges and universities. When cultural, institutional, and individual discrimination are combined, the effects on individuals and groups of individuals can be devastating to students and their ability to learn.

Researchers in the multicultural field talk about *cultural mismatches* when teachers and students come from different backgrounds and have different world views (Banks, 1997; Gay, 2000; Nieto, 2000). The more different in cultural backgrounds, the more likely individuals and groups will face cultural conflicts resulting from those differences, especially when sensitive topics or cultural incidents occur. The majority of teachers in K–12 classrooms are European American, middle class, and female (at least in the elementary grades where patterns are established), while students have increasingly diverse backgrounds. At the university level, the male/female ratio of instructors might be more balanced, but disciplines traditionally considered for one sex or the other still show gender imbalances. For instance, the fields of nursing and education usually have more women than men as both instructors and students while the fields of business and engineering are dominated by males. Lately, the number of foreign-born instructors has increased, and their backgrounds and expectations of students can contribute to cultural mismatches.

Mismatches leading to conflicts are commonplace in K–12 classrooms, especially when teachers are not sensitive to cultural differences and their implications. Inequitable patterns of teacher-student and student-student interactions established in earlier years of education are too often continued at the university level. Even if instructors do not deliberately favor individuals or groups of students, their unexamined behaviors often fall into patterns that give an advantage to some students and a disadvantage to others. Overcoming such discriminatory barriers adds to the workload of instructors initially, but provides more genuine learning environments in the long run.

NECESSARY CHANGES IN TEACHING

As a result of the changes in today's college students and what they need to succeed in the classrooms and in life, instructors need to change the way that they teach the subject matter and the discipline content so as to be more inclusive in their teaching processes. Inclusive college instructors recognize that previous ways of teaching will not be effective with this new generation of college students. They recognize that learners have many ways of demonstrating their understanding of the content and linking that content to their prior knowledge. Exciting research about learning and the brain has already influenced the way teachers think about their learners, and that research is expanding every day. Auditory and visual language learning (see Ch. 6 for further discussion), learning styles, and multiple intelligences are among the new ways of thinking about learning. College students who have worked with K–12 teachers using this new knowledge will expect their college instructors also to incorporate this knowledge into their teaching strategies.

Learning styles have been defined as the preferred ways an individual takes in and processes information (Grinder, 1991). They are the cognitive, affective, and physiological traits that each person consistently follows in interactions with the learning environment, whether reacting to new information, processing it, or responding to it. Research about learning styles and the value of teaching to them has been mixed (Grant, 1992; Irvine & York, 1995), but researchers agree with the overall concept that individuals learn differently. Dunn and Dunn's Learning Styles Inventory (Dunn, Dunn, & Price, 1978) measures certain learning styles for potential success in the classroom. Gregorc's Style Delineator (1985) categorizes learning styles on four predetermined dimensions: concrete sequential, abstract sequential, concrete random, and abstract random. Another viewpoint of learning styles is field independent learners who are able to isolate discrete factual information from the context and field dependent learners who need the surrounding contextual information for their more holistic understanding of content. One more type of learning style is global/analytical perceptions (Guild & Garger, 1985) held by holistic thinkers. This type is very similar to the concept of field dependent learners.

Closely related to learning styles is what Gardner (1997) has termed *multiple intelligences* as opposed to the traditional concept of a fixed intelligence. He feels that intelligence must be considered as the potential to process information within cultural contexts to solve problems and create products of value within those contexts. So far he has identified nine different ways individuals process and demonstrate intelligence: verbal/linguistic, logical/mathematical, musical, visual/spatial, bodily/kinesthetic, interpersonal, intrapersonal, naturalist, and existentialist. Gardner's theory gives instructors another way of engaging students in course content. From his theory, then, instructors can expect students with diverse backgrounds will process information differently. When applying Gardner's theory to the college classroom, inclusive college instructors must shift their role to facilitate the learning of all of their students, regardless of perceived ability.

INCLUSION OF ALL STUDENTS

Mismatches can often occur between an instructor and the students' styles or manner of learning. Instructors must alter their ways of teaching to include all students, not just the ones who fit previous ideal images of good students. Instructors must engage all students in the learning process and must actively involve them in the classroom setting and the course content. As mentioned earlier, inclusion is the approach to teaching so all students can process and understand the material in whatever ways are best for them. Inclusive education is a core belief and a set of teaching practices that supports the belief that all students should be full members of the community, according to Sapon-Shevin (2007). Inclusive Schools give us opportunities to practice our best selves as teachers and instructors. Inclusion can be challenging, but it is worth the effort. Inclusive instructors realize that they are responsible for providing a learning environment for all students, even those who are struggling. They understand that their beliefs, values, attitudes, and behaviors set the tone for each class and course. They know that all students can learn, and they are determined to reach all students.

Understanding these students' needs and perceptions is a major task for instructors. One tool to understanding the needs of all learners is the Learning Skills Inventory (see Table 1.1). Using this inventory can be very helpful to instructors, particularly if administered prior to the beginning of the course. In one way, instructors are better armed for this than ever before because so much more is known psychologically about teaching and learning. In another way, however, instructors have a greater pressure on them because of that knowledge. Instructors can even send such an inventory via a course management system, such as Blackboard or Angel (see ch. 9 for further discussion), as an automatic message upon registration. The results can be used by the inclusive college instructor in the overall planning of the course. However, it is essential for inclusive college instructors to safeguard the personal information of all students in an ethical manner that fits with college policies.

Armed with the concept of inclusion as the major goal, instructors must take the necessary step of analyzing the content of their subject matter. Each major concept should be analyzed for the level of difficulty in reading, writing, understanding, discussing, and other aspects of the learning process. These concepts can then be scaffolded (see Ch. 5 for further discussion) so as to teach in a manner that aids student understanding. The concept of scaffolding (Bruner, 1975) is based on the work of Vygotsky, who proposed that with an adult's assistance, children could accomplish tasks that they ordinarily could not perform independently. When applied to the college classroom, scaffolding becomes the sequencing of learning of

TABLE 1.1. Learning Styles Inventory

Name:
Date:
Directions: Please answer the following questions as honestly and as thoroughly as possible in the time given. Your responses will help me to tailor this course to meet the needs of all the learners.

1.	What background do you have in this content? Classes in high school? Outside experience? Volunteer or paid employment? None?
2.	Is this course required? *Yes No* In registering for this class, how did you feel? Anxious? Curious? Excited? Why?
3.	How do you learn best? Hands on? Visually? By listening? Writing your own notes? Repetition?
4.	What type of assessment best shows your learning? Actual performance? Open-ended responses such as short or long essay? Closed-ended questioning such as multiple choice or True and False? Other?
5.	What other information do you feel I as your instructor need to know about you?

difficult tasks, orchestrated by the instructor who is the expert. The materials are taught in that prepared sequence so learners can understand and absorb difficult and complex concepts throughout the learning process.

Scaffolding in instruction is the instructor's use of supports and systematic sequencing of content and materials to optimize learning. Scaffolding is a process in which students are given support until they can apply new skills and strategies independently (Rosenshine & Meister, 1994). When students are learning new or difficult tasks, they are given more assistance as directed by the instructor. As they begin to demonstrate task mastery, the assistance or support is decreased gradually in order to shift the responsibility for learning from the instructor to the students. Thus, as the students assume more responsibility for their learning, the instructor provides less support and takes on the role of facilitator. In the college classroom, it is critical that inclusive college instructors consider the use of scaffolding in the curriculum, in instruction, and in assessment.

Curriculum

For curriculum concerns, one powerful technique is personalizing whatever is being taught. That means relating the content to students' prior knowledge, specifically their cultural experiences. Unfortunately, the curriculum for many university courses is still based on European American historical, political, economic and cultural experiences. For students who are not European American, finding themselves or their cultural backgrounds and experiences in the curriculum might be a rare occasion. Inclusive instructors, however, use examples from a variety of cultures, presenting alternative viewpoints and ways of knowing. This form of scaffolding needs to be a conscious approach to viewing the course content from multiple perspectives.

One way to use students' personal and cultural connections to course content is having students find Internet articles and/or interview family members and community leaders. In a graduate education course recently, students were asked to investigate a highly-valued artifact or skill that they inherited or developed. One student reported on her African American heritage of quilt-making while another described his telephone interview with a locally-known Native American storyteller. Although the student himself was European American, he liked to use storytelling in his classes, and the interview gave him further insights into this oral art. Additions to and modifications of the curriculum need to be reinforced by giving them adequate instructional time. These changes should also be included in the assessment process. In the example above, students shared what they learned and were later tested on what others contributed to class discussions.

Instruction

For instructional approaches, teaching strategies need to be varied and to take into account the learning styles and the multiple intelligences (Gardner, 1997) of students. All of these learning styles and intelligences can suggest a wide variety of possibilities for instructors to present course content. In higher education, instructors tend to use lecture-recitation patterns and to rely upon students' linguistic and logical-mathematical abilities for processing the desired quantity of information. Yet many students do not learn well under such conditions and need more active and personal connections to the material. Although Power Point slides have added the visual dimension to lecturing, they can be too cluttered with information or too many to retain the attention of all students. Also, the recitation type of questioning asks for factual, short-answer responses and usually engages only a few of the students.

Employing a combination of modalities such as visual, auditory, and kinesthetic is one way to get students more actively involved. Power Point lectures can include illustrations, photos, or video clips. In order to have students interact with the material and each other, however, the Power

Points should include challenging questions that require individual and small group reflection and discussion. One technique for individual response is called a quick-write where every student must respond on a 3 × 5 card within a minute or so. The cards are then passed forward and collected. Instructors can use these for checking students' understanding as a group or as individuals. A relatively new technique, beneficial particularly for large classes, is the use of student electronic clickers (see Ch. 7 for further discussion) that register each student's answer to a yes/no or multiple-choice question and then tabulates all responses for the whole class to see. Clicker responses can also be used with small-group discussion by having pre-planned groups discuss the answer and respond as a group.

Using cooperative learning groups is an excellent way to get students interacting with each other in a productive manner, according to its proponents (Johnson & Johnson, 1994). With cooperative groups, each individual must have a role that contributes to the group goal. Roles such as leader, recorder, reporter, and group-process observer are common choices, and can be rotated within groups on a regular basis. Without individual responsibilities, small-group discussions or activities too often become dominated by one or two individuals with the loss of some students' viewpoints. Well-planned cooperative learning tasks, on the other hand, can lead to a wide variety of responses and contributions from students who ordinarily keep quiet in whole-class discussions.

One added advantage to cooperative learning groups as a teaching strategy is its congruence with various cultural practices. For cultures that tend to be communal, with an emphasis on group collaboration rather than individual achievement, cooperative learning with predetermined roles complements the preferred mode of working and sharing in the family and community. Using cooperative learning groups within the classroom and encouraging cooperative study groups outside the classroom can provide students with mental challenges and emotional support as well as different perspectives regarding the course content and assignments.

Assessment

With the change in students and the need for a corresponding change in instructors, the classroom climate regarding assessment also has to change. Students are less tolerant of what they perceive as a meaningless classroom environment removed from real life. They are demanding that learning be directly related to the knowledge and skills necessary to compete in the technological workplace of the information age. Therefore, the classroom environment must to some extent mimic the workplace yet go beyond this to create independent thinkers who can also critique the workplace. The interconnectedness is best viewed as a dynamic triangle of students, instructor, and the assessment process.

Cultural and institutional forms of discrimination are demonstrated by practices such as the high reliance on traditional assessments of papers and tests. The standardized testing used by the No Child Left Behind legislation tends to favor students who have had strong academic backgrounds. Scholastic Achievement Test (SAT) and Achievement College Test (ACT) scores reveal similar flaws. Perhaps as predictors of traditional university instruction and assessment, they have had some success, but the danger is that these tests do not demonstrate what all types of learners know and can do. Fortunately, universities are realizing this to some degree and are looking beyond standardized test scores to diversify student populations. If, however, traditional methods of assessment such as papers and tests are still the most common ways of finding out what students have learned, these same students who struggled with SATs and ACTs will again be disadvantaged.

Instructors need to consider other assessment methods, especially when some of these methods more closely resemble what the students will be expected to do in their careers. For instance, usually the best assessment of pre-service teachers is student teaching when they take full charge of classrooms. In addition to evaluating real-life tasks, such authentic assessments also fit the learning styles of many students today. Students who are field-dependent appreciate the learning of content knowledge and skills in actual contexts where their street-smarts abilities come into play. Often these students, who struggle with lecture-mode learning and multiple-choice assessment, perform as well or better than field-independent students because they are able to apply their intuitive senses.

Field experiences or internships related to courses are not always possible or practical, but other forms of authentic assessment methods can include portfolios, projects, and presentations. Providing examples through field experiences or internships when possible helps many students see theories more clearly. Case studies and anecdotal records are important when real life experiences are not possible, and can be introduced through readings and small-group discussions. Cooperative learning projects, presentations, and portfolios are some possibilities using alternative assessment methods. Inclusive college instructors should be flexible enough to accept alternative assessments when special cases arise.

CONCLUSIONS

Today, schools in the United States are buffeted by constant demands for results that may not be easily administered. As Ainscow (2008) recognizes, teaching and learning are not conducted in a vacuum, and choices are made by a variety of individuals who impact the learners both inside and outside the classroom. College instructors are in the position of power over their students since they control the curriculum, the instruction, and—most significantly—the assessment. Rarely are college instructors' grades overturned by higher authorities. Students have some power as a group with student evaluations of instructors, but such power is usually cumulative over several semesters and even then is only one of many factors affecting instructors' retention and promotion. Inclusive college instructors, therefore, have the primary responsibility to create within their classrooms environments conducive to learning.

Inclusive college instructors understand that such a student-friendly environment requires work and vigilance on their part. They make every attempt to avoid using their ultimate power to harm students and/or prevent learning from taking place. They work to avoid or minimize individual, cultural, and institutional discrimination by being sensitive to situations and relationships. They constantly explore ways to build professional and personal connections with their students, seeing these as whole people with lives beyond the classroom. Inclusive college instructors know that out-of-school cultural connections are an underlying part of every classroom and can affect, positively or negatively, the learning community of the classroom. Most important, inclusive college instructors embrace student diversity as something that will enrich the learning community, students and instructors alike.

This book is a practical approach for reaching and teaching all students in college classrooms. The emphasis is on the inclusive nature of the college classroom community, building the learning environment to meet the varying backgrounds and needs of all students. The changing face of college students today requires a shift in the thinking and instructional strategies of college professors, regardless of their discipline or content area. What follows in these chapters are practical strategies for understanding the learners, teaching the discipline and creating a classroom environment conducive to learning of all. Readers are encouraged to try these strategies, and to change or adapt them for use in various disciplines. The scholarship of teaching requires all college instructors to systematically look at their teaching and to become more effective in today's college classrooms. The key to success for instructors is to become inclusive, welcoming and supporting all students and the richness of their diversity.

REFERENCES

Ainscow, M. (2008). Teaching for diversity: The next big challenge. In M. Connelly, M. F. He, & J. Phillion (Eds.) *The Sage Handbook of Curriculum and Instruction.* (pp. 240–258). Los Angeles: Sage.

Banks, J. (1997). *Educating citizens in a multicultural society.* New York: Teachers College Press.

Brown, S. C., & Kysilka, M. L. (2002). *Applying multicultural and global concepts in the classroom and beyond.* Boston, MA: Allyn & Bacon.

Bruner, J. (1975). Poverty and childhood. *Oxford Education Review,1,*(1), 31–50.

Dunn, R., Dunn, K., & Price, G. E. (1978). *Learning styles inventory.* Lawrence, KS: Price Systems.

Gardner, H. (1997). *Beyond multiple intelligences.* Keynote speech at the annual meeting of the Association for the Supervision and Curriculum Development. San Antonio, March 22.

Gay, G. (2000). *Culturally responsive teaching: Theory, research, and practice.* New York: Teachers College Press.

Grant, C. (Ed.) (1992). *Research and multicultural education: From the margins to the mainstream.* Washington, DC: Falmer Press.

Gregorc, A. (1985). *Gregorc style lineator.* Maynard, MA: Gabriel Systems.

Grinder. M. (1991). *Righting the educational conveyor belt.* Portland, OR: Metamorphous Press.

Guild, P. B., & Garger, S. (1985). Marching to different drummers. Alexandria, VA: Association for Supervision and Curriculum Development. Jacobson, S., (2002). *Education about education with neurolinguistic programming. Lincoln, NE: iUniverse.*

Irvine, J. J., & York, D. E. (1995). Learning styles and culturally diverse students: A literature review. In J. Banks & C. Banks (Eds.), *Handbook of research on multicultural education* (pp. 484-497). New York: Macmillan.

Johnson, D., & Johnson, R. (1994). *Learning together and alone.* Boston: Allyn & Bacon.

Koppelman, K. L., & Goodhart, R. L. (2008). *Understanding human differences: Multicultural education for a diverse America* (3rd ed.). Boston, MA: Allyn & Bacon.

Kunc, N. (1992). The need to belong: Rediscovering Maslow's hierarchy of needs. In R. Villa, J. Thousand, W. Stainback, & S. Stainback (Eds.). *Restructuring for caring and effective education.* (pp. 37–40). Baltimore: Paul Brookes.

Nieto, S. (2000). *Affirming diversity: The sociopolitical context of multicultural education* (3rd ed.). New York: Longman.

Rosenshine, B., & Meister, C., (1994). Reciprocal teaching: A review of the research. *Review of Educational Research, 64,* 479–530.

Sapon-Shevin, M., (2007). *Widening the circle: The power of inclusive classrooms.* Boston, MA: Beacon Press.

CHAPTER 2

STUDENTS AS CULTURAL BEINGS

Susan C. Brown

KEY TERMS

Communal Cultures; High-context Culture; Low-context Culture; *No Child Left Behind*; Multicultural and Global Education; Polychronic Cultures

REFLECTIVE QUESTIONS

- What knowledge, skills, and dispositions are essential for cultural competence?
- How can an instructor's cultural competence help overcome discrimination in the classroom?
- Why are professional and personal interactions at the heart of being culturally competent?

INTRODUCTION

Today's university students in the United States are more diverse culturally than ever before. As mentioned in Chapter 1, cultural differences include age, race/ethnicity, social class, sex, language, religion, sexual orientation, ability of mind or body, regionality (U.S. location influences), and national-

Teaching Inclusively in Higher Education, pages 17–37
Copyright © 2010 by Information Age Publishing
17

ity. Historically, some college instructors may remember when certain students were not served in public schools. Those times are long gone and federal laws now protect the rights of today's college students. College instructors who wish to become inclusive in their teaching need to recognize, honor, and use knowledge of student diversity in order to enrich student learning of course content. Recognizing a student as an English language learner is a start. Honoring that student's need for additional exam time and assistance with certain grammatical structures, or the student's difficulty in expressing an opinion in class shows more concern and involvement in the student's learning. Using knowledge of a student's cultural background, worldview, and ways of doing things shows even more commitment to the student's success in the course.

In college courses crowded with seemingly essential content knowledge, making room for various student experiences seems like one more burden to many instructors. Yet taking time to include all students and honor all students' contributions very often saves time in the end. Included students are more likely to be involved students, ones who actively participate in the learning process. How to use the cultural backgrounds and contributions of all students to enrich course content and the learning process must be an essential task for instructors. A major part of inclusivity is what instructors do to overcome discrimination found at all levels of education. Inclusive instructors make all students feel welcomed and valued for their contributions to the learning community of the classroom.

INSTRUCTORS' OWN CULTURAL BACKGROUNDS

Inclusive college instructors wishing success for all students embrace diversity not as just a nice idea, but as a working condition. To do this, they first need to examine themselves and their teaching to see how their beliefs, values, attitudes, and behaviors influence the students' learning. The Cultural Concept Map (Brown & Kysilka, 2002, p. 27) has individuals identifying themselves according to cultural groups (see Table 2.1).

The cultural groups, each in a circle, are age, race/ethnicity, social class, gender, sexual orientation, language, religion, disability, regionality, and nationality. For each culture, a descriptive word or phrase can be attached. For example, the words *middle class* might be used to describe individuals' perceptions of their social and economic status. Beyond each cultural circle with its descriptive phrase individuals can add beliefs or feelings that influence them. For example, connected to middle class might be anyone can make it if he/she works hard enough. Instructors themselves can use the Cultural Concept Map designed for students by changing the words *learning* and *learn* to *teaching* and *teach*. Examining personal cultural circles and

TABLE 2.1.   Cultural Concept Map

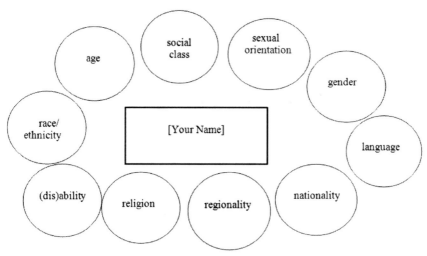

Directions:

1.   Fill in each of the cultural circles with a descriptor to identify yourself. Do not feel obligated to fill in all circles, but if you leave some blank, consider why.

2.   Choose one cultural circle that might affect your learning in this class. For that cultural circle, note influences such as customs, beliefs, values, and family or friends:

3.   Consider how these influences might affect your learning of course content. In what ways might they help and/or hinder your ability to learn?

4.   Make an action plan based on your findings. What simple and doable steps can you take to succeed this semester?

Adapted from Brown, S. & Kysilka, M. (2002). Applying multicultural and global concepts in the classroom and beyond. Boston: Allyn & Bacon.

their influences can help inclusive college instructors recognize similar and different influences in others.

The point of the Cultural Concept Map is to identify underlying core beliefs and values that define each individual. With their own cultural backgrounds brought to the foreground, inclusive college instructors are more likely to see potential points of conflict with their students' beliefs and values. As college instructors think about their position of privilege in the classroom and the larger world, they might see how being middle-class and well-educated with career status already gives them social status over many if not all students. Adding race, gender, language and/or other cultural backgrounds that represent the dominant culture puts instructors in a strongly dominating position. Most college instructors can remember isolated times and events where they were discriminated against, but few have had persistent and pervasive experiences of discrimination over the

TABLE 2.2. Instructor Self-Assessment in Multicultural and Global Education

KEY: 1=Almost Always 2 =Frequently 3=Occasionally 4=Almost Never 5=Not Applicable

A. Personal/Professional Development

1. I feel comfortable discussing racial issues with people of other races as well as my own. 1 2 3 4 5

2. I read books or articles to increase my understanding of the particular aspirations and frustrations of people with diverse cultural backgrounds. 1 2 3 4 5

3. I maintain personal associations which reflect diversity of all types (age, race, sex, sexual orientation, religion, ableness, regionality, nationality, etc.) 1 2 3 4 5

4. I stay informed about international events and recognize their importance in my life and my students' lives. 1 2 3 4 5

5. I have the professional training needed to work effectively with people with diverse cultural backgrounds. 1 2 3 4 5

6. I use my colleagues' expertise to extend my own knowledge of and skills in multicultural and global concepts. 1 2 3 4 5

B. Awareness and Sensitivity

7. I am conscious of cultural differences in such areas as communicating with people of other cultural groups. 1 2 3 4 5

8. I encourage diversity of values, lifestyles, and viewpoints even when these run counter to my own preferences. 1 2 3 4 5

9. I take the initiative in dispelling prejudices, stereotypes, and misconceptions among students. 1 2 3 4 5

10. I recognize my own cultural biases and try to see issues from other viewpoints. 1 2 3 4 5

11. I try to prevent any prejudiced or stereotyped thinking from unfairly influencing my expectations of students. 1 2 3 4 5

C. Curriculum Content

12. I promote conservation and ecological concern in the classroom. 1 2 3 4 5

13. I give my students opportunities to express, celebrate, and maintain cultural differences. 1 2 3 4 5

14. I use a multicultural/global approach and appropriate materials to teach course content. 1 2 3 4 5

15. I stress the interdependence of nations and people around the world, relating world events to local communities. 1 2 3 4 5

16. I develop student skills and values necessary for survival in the dominant culture without denying other values equally appropriate in non-dominant cultures. 1 2 3 4 5

(*continued*)

TABLE 2.2. continued

D. Curriculum Resources

17. I know where to obtain multicultural/global materials that are free of   1 2 3 4 5
cultural biases for use in my courses.

18. I have evaluated my textbooks to determine whether they contain fair and 1 2 3 4 5
appropriate treatment of persons from all cultural groups (including age,
race, sex, sexual orientation, religion, age, disability, nationality)

19. The materials that I use about diverse cultural groups are an integral part 1 2 3 4 5
of the curriculum rather than just attached or treated separately.

20. I regularly bring in extra multicultural/global materials to supplement   1 2 3 4 5
the curriculum.

E. Instruction

21. I model for my students respect, openness, and honesty in   1 2 3 4 5
communications and encourage them to do the same.

22. I search for ways to overcome the reluctance of students to recognize and 1 2 3 4 5
discuss diversity issues and questions.

23. I adjust my teaching methodologies with students with diverse   1 2 3 4 5
backgrounds, interests, and needs.

24. I clearly demonstrate that academic expectations are equally high for   1 2 3 4 5
students from all cultural backgrounds.

25. I use cooperative learning groups with planned combinations of students 1 2 3 4 5
of different sexes, abilities, and other cultural backgrounds.

26. I provide opportunities for students to interact and learn from each other 1 2 3 4 5
regularly during class periods.

F. Community Relations

27. I seek the assistance of local communities along with the Internet in   1 2 3 4 5
developing multicultural and global activities.

28. I have visited and familiarized myself with the local communities of my   1 2 3 4 5
students.

29. I have attended social, religious, or cultural events held by members of my 1 2 3 4 5
students' communities.

30. I use community members from various cultural backgrounds as visiting   1 2 3 4 5
lecturers and/or resource people.

(modified from Brown & Kysilka, 2002)

years. Yet many of their students experience discrimination regularly. For these students, and for all students, inclusive college instructors must take care to be empathetic towards them and their lives, inside and out of the classroom.

Another self assessment inclusive instructors can use to gain more insight into their teaching is the Instructor Self Assessment for Multicultural and Global Education (see Table 2.2), modified from Brown and Kysilka's original assessment (2002, pp. 52–53).

Although the emphasis in this chapter is on information and application related to multicultural education, global education is also a part of today's college classroom. *Multicultural and global education* can be defined in the following way:

> Multicultural and global education can be seen as the educational process of acquiring new knowledge, skills, and values to participate actively in a complex, pluralistic, and interconnected society and to work together for change in individuals and institutions in order to make that world society more just and humane (Brown & Kysilka, 2002, p. 9).

Inclusive college instructors should keep in mind that these statements are expressing ideal behaviors in relationship to multicultural and global education principles and that they should see these statements as possible goals. They cannot be achieved overnight or even in a semester, but are ideals to work for over a career of teaching.

One personal aspect inclusive college instructors should consider is their openness and willingness to suspend judgment about their students and their students' cultural backgrounds. As humans, we all have prejudices about other individuals and groups. When these are not examined and when they influence behaviors, the outcomes are often discriminatory practices. Even if instructors are uncertain about students' backgrounds, they can learn to pause and think about unexpected or unusual student reactions to teacher behaviors. For instance, when a European American male instructor tried to shake hands with a new East Indian Muslim colleague, the woman did not extend her hand. In a kind way, she explained that this would be improper in her culture for her to touch him. Students who do not feel empowered enough to explain such a cultural expectation would be put in a very uncomfortable position. In cases like this, college instructors must question whether such an unusual student behavior is tied to a cultural expectation rather than taking the behavior as a deliberate insult.

STUDENTS' CULTURAL BACKGROUNDS

The most effective way for instructors to minimize discrimination in all its forms is to learn about students as individuals and as groups and then apply that knowledge to teaching and learning situations. University records available to instructors are fairly extensive, but more information can be gathered in the first few sessions of the course. Typically, instructors hand out information forms for students to fill, asking about addresses, e-mails, majors, and interests. To supplement these, forms such as the Learning Skills Inventory (refer back to Ch. 1 for additional information) can be used. Additional information can also be gathered with open-ended questions such as the following related to the topic of Becoming a Strong Student in This Course:

- What do you see as your responsibility in this course?
- What do you see as my responsibility?
- What do you see as concerns or challenges in the way of success?
- How will you try to overcome these?
- How can I help you overcome these?

These questions can first be discussed orally with the inclusive college instructor mentioning several examples such as work and family responsibilities. Students can be urged to be thoughtful and specific, with the inclusive college instructor's guarantee of privacy except in the case of legal requirements, for example, drug or alcohol use.

A modified form of the Cultural Concept Map can be used with students with the understanding that all cultural circles do not have to be filled and that any information shared would be kept confidential. Students might be asked to choose one or more of the cultural circles that have placed significant roles in their learning and their choice of career. In similar exercises, students have discussed many different cultural influences from being a person of color, to being an immigrant, to being a conservative Christian. This exercise can be done in class or as an assignment to be turned in to the instructor. The information should be kept confidential unless the specific student is willing to share. The gained knowledge about students can be used to plan or guide future classroom activities and discussions.

Inclusive college instructors need to consider each cultural influence in the context of the college course being taught. Depending upon the course, the students, and the classroom setting, inclusive college instructors can look for ways to support students' cultural diversity and personal uniqueness. Inclusive college instructors can also bridge gaps, helping students to succeed in the academic world of universities. Looking for cultural mismatches, when cultural ways of thinking and acting are different enough to cause discomfort or conflict, and proactively finding ways to overcome them are the regular practice of inclusive instructors. The next section will examine the cultural influences individually and offer suggestions of ways to work with these influences in the classroom.

Age

The wide range of ages found among today's university student population gives college instructors interesting and often overlooked ways to think about their students. Lyons, McIntosh, and Kysilka (2003) devote a chapter in their book to the major differences among three distinct generations found in universities: the Baby Boom Generation, born between 1943 and 1961; Generation X, born between 1962 and 1981; and the Millennial Generation, born between 1982 and 2000. Each generation has its own chronologically related national and international events that have profoundly influenced the worldviews for that generation. In turn, those generational worldviews are brought into the university classrooms, resulting in three distinct groupings of student attitudes and behaviors. Lyons, McIntosh, and Kysilka (2003) caution instructors to be proactive about these generational mismatches likely to be encountered when all three groups are in the same classroom.

The Baby Boom Generation

Baby Boom students, like many university instructors, experienced the effects of the Vietnam War and the deaths of Martin Luther King, Jr., and the Kennedys. They are predominantly European American. They have worked for many years, and typically have grown children and even grandchildren. Baby Boomers tend to be worried about academic assignments such as research papers, especially if they hadn't taken university courses for a long time. Yet they are determined to learn and to make up for lost opportunities when they were younger. They consider education a privilege and count on their families to support them through their academic struggles. They are respectful of college instructors and look to them as role models.

Many of the Baby Boomers' academic concerns can be addressed early in the semester by the college instructor. The use of open-ended questions is one way to get out the academic concerns of these students. Providing time before and after class for individual problems can also help. For specific assignment concerns, special mini-sessions such as ones on doing research can be held at the end of class for those who wish to attend. Whole-class sessions with research librarians are also possible if enough students need this information. Most important, Baby Boomers need recognition of the life experiences they bring to the class. They may not have written a college paper recently, but they have worked in a wide variety of companies and organizations and have dealt with life problems in family and work situations. They are also willing to work very hard to earn a high course grade, including doing extra credit or redoing an assignment. Their more pragmatic worldview balances the untested idealism of younger students. Inclusive college instructors can involve these students by asking them to make parallels between practical lessons learned over a lifetime and academic concepts and theories being presented.

Generation X Students

Generation X students experienced events such as Watergate, the end of the Cold War, boom and bust companies, and corporations with leaders of dubious morals. They are more diverse racially, especially those taking advantage of targeted scholarships. These students are more apt to be children of non-nuclear families, experiencing a wide range of household arrangements from single parenting to grand parenting or blended family. The costs of living, housing, and education have increased dramatically in their lifetime so most have worked throughout their high school and college years. They have spent more money than previous generations on personal wants that have become needs. They are familiar and comfortable with the computer and the Internet and expect instructors to entertain them as they have been entertained from their early years by Sesame Street, MTV, and violent crime and war scenes. They see college or university education as a right and college instructors as product providers.

Generation X students have less consistent academic backgrounds than previous generations and are especially weak in written expression. Many had to take remedial courses before being accepted into university. These students are the first generation to grow up with technology as an integral part of their lives. They are often not as focused or industrious as the Baby Boomers before them. College instructors have the role of persuading these students that serious effort needs to be put into course work, including sufficient time outside class. Several ways can be used to persuade these students to attend class, among them having a short written assignment or quick quiz each period. One instructor has his students write and turn in a one-page response to a prompt given to them during the previous class. Another has students answer briefly one of the questions found at the end of each text chapter reading assignment. Inclusive college instructors have also used cooperative learning groups with different students responsible each class for leading a small-group discussion based on the readings. The point is to make each student individually responsible for showing up and being prepared for class. For students with grammatical problems, inclusive college instructors can make checklists explaining common errors found in their disciplines. Students are then made responsible for using the checklist. Students with serious problems can be referred to the writing center found on most campuses. Some college instructors require all students to attend at least one session at the center before submitting a major term paper.

The Millennial Students

The Millennial students, the youngest generation on campus, have been shaped by 9/11, the war on terrorism, and *No Child Left Behind*, (federally-mandated legislation tying funds to state standardized testing). They are the most diverse group on campus racially and economically. Increasing numbers of Latinos/as have made this the largest group of people of color, outnumbering African Americans for the first time. At the graduate level particularly, more Chinese, Indian, other Asians, and students of diverse ethnicities from the former Soviet Union areas are attending American universities. Millennial students have experienced high-stakes testing and academic pressure throughout their K–12 school years. They grew up with computers and technology and would find it difficult to function without cell phones, iPods, and the like. However, due to financial inequities, not every student has the same access to the same technology. Not as focused and appreciative as Baby Boom students, yet not as self-serving and individualistic as Generation X students, Millennial students expect to compete but also work together, in university as well as in later life. They see college education as a means to an economic end rather than an end in itself, and they are willing to do what it takes to succeed.

Millennial students are used to academic pressure so will expect that. At the same time, they have busy lives with jobs, active social calendars, and often family responsibilities as children and/or parents. They want to know up front what course assignments and expectations their college instructors have, and will drop courses or switch sections if they feel their needs will not be met. Like Generation X students, they also might struggle with written work. Instructors for these students must be ready to use technology such as Power Point presentations. A significant number of students do not read the course texts, expecting the Power Point handouts to cover all the essential content and to serve as study guides. One possible solution for inclusive college instructors is to provide an outline form and expect students to fill it in during class. Another way is to use Power Point for background information only while expecting students to do other readings or find related articles for whole-class or small-group discussions. However technology is used, in-class activities applying major concepts are essential for students to process the new knowledge in a meaningful way.

Lyons, McIntosh, and Kysilka (2003) make a good case for seeing today's college students as diverse because of the generational differences. Yet several other very important factors influence individual students and their interactions among themselves and with instructors. Inclusive college instructors remind themselves that each individual is not only a member of different cultural groups such as age, class, and race, but also a unique person who will respond in his or her own way to the complex environment of a university classroom.

Race

European American students are still the most common racial groups on campus. Asian/Asian American students continue to have a strong presence. Recent scholarships targeting underrepresented groups of students have resulted in more African American, Latino/a, and Native American students in the university population. Efforts by university administrations, concerned with low retention rates of students of color, have resulted in multicultural centers and support services. This may include efforts such as mentoring by college instructors of color. Even with these recent efforts, U.S. universities are not always welcoming places for students of color.

Being a racial minority on campus means being the target for all three forms of discrimination (refer back to Ch. 1 for additional information). Individual racism is seen in the overt form of racial slurs, name-calling, and occasionally physical harassment and the more subtle form of stereotyping groups or ignoring or not including individuals. When considering cultural discrimination, European American instructors especially have a responsibility to examine ways they have been favored throughout their own education (Sleeter & McLaren, 1995). They need to be aware of how societal privileges for their dominant culture influence the dynamics of classrooms and higher education institutions. Institutional discrimination is more difficult to recognize, but it shows up in practices such as hiring international professors who speak only standard English and have preferred accents, British being the most acceptable.

Inclusive college instructors need to be aware of the special concerns of students of color and be ready to provide help and information about appropriate resources. College instructors' lack of awareness about racial discrimination can adversely affect learning for students of color, in turn leading to high dropout rates (Howard, 1999). As Gay (1994) states, "If students believe that the college environment is alien and hostile toward them or does not value who they are (as many students of color believe), they will not be able to concentrate as thoroughly as they might on academic tasks" (Gay, 1994, p. 9).

Inclusive college instructors can help students of color by being sensitive to their situations in class. Students of color often sit next to each other, sometimes by choice and sometimes by default when white students avoid sitting next to them. Moving students into different cooperative groups is one way to encourage a wider range of interactions among students. This has the disadvantage, however, of moving students out of their preferred location in the room so inclusive instructors should be ready for some resistance initially. Along with physical isolation, students of color might be psychologically isolated by being expected to represent their race's position, particularly in discussions about societal issues and problems. On most issues, a wide range of perspectives and opinions can be found within racial groups. Expecting students to give a collective perspective for their races is putting the students and racial groups into an "us versus them" relationship, further isolating the students. These students' viewpoints are extremely important, however, and they should be encouraged to participate as individuals as well as representatives of specific groups.

Gender

The effects of cultural sexism can be seen very early, even in preschool children. Girls are expected by society to be more docile, concerned about appearances, and dependent while boys are expected to be more rough-and-tumble, adventuresome, and independent according to researchers such as Sadker and Sadker (1994) and the American Association for University Women (AAUW, 1992, 1998). By the time they enter kindergarten, boys and girls have already absorbed many attitudes and behaviors that are expected according to their sex. In kindergarten to Grade 12 classrooms, these cultural forms of discrimination become institutionalized. Girls are less likely to be called upon, less likely to be asked difficult questions, and less likely to get helpful and encouraging feedback for their responses than boys (Sadker & Sadker, 1994; AAUW, 1992, 1998). They also are less likely to be encouraged by teachers and counselors to pursue courses leading to careers in science and math. This institutionalized form of discrimination continues in university, affecting the distribution of sexes in courses as well as the behavior of instructors and students in classrooms. Women dominate in the caring professions such as teaching, social work, and health, while men continue to dominate in other areas such as engineering, science, and mathematics.

In university classrooms, if college instructors fall into similar patterns of encouraging one sex over the other through sexist comments or behaviors, they reinforce what societal and institutional policies and practices have been teaching—that one group is inferior to the other. Inclusive instructors can monitor their own calling-on patterns, by using a random system such as individual name cards or noting down on a class list who volunteered and who was called on to answer instructor questions. As a general practice, inclusive college instructors can also insist upon hearing from diverse voices by asking for those who haven't yet answered to speak up. That puts both the eager volunteers and the quiet students on warning about who is to respond next. The so-called Jeopardy players—those students who are first to respond to any question and often call out—must be reminded to slow down and think before speaking out. One way to do this is to ask divergent, challenging questions that require more than simple factual answers and then to allow for appropriate wait time, at least three to five seconds between asking the question and calling upon an individual. Allowing additional time to think, translate, and process information can be a valuable help to students with learning problems as well as students for whom English is not their first language. Monitoring of cooperative learning groups is also important since white men tend to dominate, particularly if they are older with leadership experience and a let's get it done approach to assignments. Even the use of roles in cooperative learning groups can be ignored by students if not insisted upon and supervised by inclusive college instructors.

Social Class

More students from working class and poor families are attending college today. Many reasons contribute to this influx of students. Scholarships such as those for first-generation college students are much more common. Counselors in high schools and community colleges are more knowledgeable about opportunities for high achieving students. The abundance of community colleges has also contributed to the changing college population, since students with personal and family financial responsibilities are now more able to combine work and education while living at home. Evening and weekend classes along with the regular day classes offer these students flexibility in scheduling, particularly at the large universities where several sections of the same course are offered each semester.

The challenge with these students for inclusive college instructors is to help them overcome economic and social barriers. Schubert (as cited in Brown, Mir, & Warner, 1996, p. 348) mentions that educators interpret educational needs and problems of students and their families through middle-class lens and do not have much empathy for those on the boundaries. The high cost of textbooks and technological tools can be prohibitive to certain students, especially if multiple texts are required for the course. Inclusive college instructors can help by putting text copies on reserve at the university library and allowing students to purchase older editions of the text online. Sometimes students do not receive their financial grants before classes start, but inclusive college instructors can help by having text copies that can be loaned out for the first few weeks. Inclusive instructors can also facilitate student sharing of texts where feasible and possible.

Family emergencies sometimes interfere with students' ability to attend class or turn in an assignment on time. Most college instructors examine each situation with the individual student and then decide to make exceptions when genuine emergencies have happened. Often, however, what is considered an emergency to a student is not one to the instructor. Family obligations are interpreted differently by social class and by race and ethnicity. Working class families and families in poverty tend to depend upon each other for entertainment and emotional and financial support. *Communal cultures*—those with acknowledged and honored extended family ties—often demand more of relatives, expecting members to attend family events such as holidays, birthdays, or even births and operations, and to be in touch constantly. Not to attend or stay in close touch is an insult to the family. One 40-year-old Latina mentioned that she talked with her mother at least once a day, and sometimes two or three times. Inclusive college instructors will make their expectations of attendance clear from the start of the course, but will be considerate about what students perceive as an emergency. One method is to allow one or two absences per semester and to remind students to save these for possible emergencies.

Language

Increasing Latino/a, foreign, and immigrant student populations mean that most instructors will have several students whose command of conversational and/or academic English is not strong. Although international students are required to pass a language exam, they might have enough reading and writing skills to pass while still not being able to follow fast-flowing conversations and classroom discussions. In addition, students who do not speak standard English at home might also have difficulty expressing themselves orally and in written form. Reading many textbook pages can be difficult for these students, as well as for other students lacking the highly academic language skills needed for university work. Even if comprehension of the material is not a problem, the difficulty of expressing knowledge might mask a student's true understanding of the course content. Unfortunately, most college instructors, like their counterparts in K–12, are fluent only in English so do not understand the demands of doing academic work in another language (Zimpher, 1989).

Inclusive college instructors can help students to accomplish longer and more complex assignments by dividing large assignments into parts with different deadlines. For instance, insisting upon topic choice, then outline, then rough draft and final copy deadlines for papers will push students to plan and organize research and writing earlier. This also gives inclusive instructors several chances to give constructive feedback that will hopefully lead to higher student success rates. Using rubrics and scoring guides, students can also self-assess their progress and product. One way to cut down on required reading material while still covering the content is to have various groups of students present different chapters or supplementary articles to the class along with handouts and challenging follow-up questions. Some college instructors might worry about giving too much assistance, but tough expectations can still be set as long as the quality of the learning product is stressed rather than the quantity of content covered.

Religion

Christianity is still the major religion in the U.S., but that broad category ranges from fundamentalist to liberal and non-denominational groups. American and international Muslims are under a good deal of pressure since 9/11 to demonstrate their loyalty. University environments are less welcoming now to men who look Middle Eastern, especially if they are Muslim. In a more subtle ways, however, universities show institutional discrimination against non-Christian students. Calendar years, for instance, are planned for breaks during Christmas. Calling this a winter break instead of a Christmas one does not disguise its original purpose of allowing Christians time for the family holiday. Holy days for other religions, on the other hand, are for the most part ignored.

Inclusive college instructors can acknowledge important holidays for various religions during the semester by first checking a calendar that lists major religious holidays before planning the course schedule. This will help prevent putting tests on days that are special to various religions. Inclusive instructors can find ways for students to make up missing class and can provide class notes, activity materials, and quizzes to students by e-mail. Inclusive college instructors can also learn about holy days that might affect student performance. For instance, the holy month for Muslims is Ramadan, located on the western calendar at different times of the year according to the Islamic lunar calendar. During this month, devout adult Muslims regularly fast from sunrise to sunset so Muslim students might seem tired and lethargic in class. Inclusive instructors will understand the importance of religious holidays, what is to be expected, and how they can avoid penalizing any of their students for their beliefs.

A sensitive area concerning religion is the argument of evolution versus creationism or intelligent design. College instructors in the sciences particularly might have students who resist western scientific data about the age of the universe or the planet Earth and its first inhabitants. It can be very difficult to present the scientific evidence while allowing for the possibility of other perspectives. Respecting students and their perspectives will take patience, yet not demonstrating this respect will certainly lead to alienating the students. Agreeing to disagree might be the most desirable outcome, avoiding painful confrontational classroom situations.

Sexual Orientation

Although homophobia is still a problem on campuses as well as in the general American society, students are more open today about their sexuality and generally more accepting of others' different sexual orientations.

Some gay instructors and students feel comfortable being out whereas doing so in past decades often put them at risk. Yet being out can result in targeted discriminatory practices such as avoidance or harassment. Many gay students are reluctant to reveal their sexuality and choose to remain silent even when their perspectives on social issues would be valuable.

Inclusive instructors can help gay, lesbian, bisexual, and transgender students by being supportive when issues of sexuality are part of the course content. Straight college instructors can be advocates for gay-straight alliances on campus and elsewhere such as PFLAG (Parents and Friends of Lesbians and Gays). They can encourage all students to attend lectures and events on sexuality such as diversity week presentations. They can use true stories about gay experiences, especially ones that are contemporary. One college instructor regularly talks about a gay students' panel she attended where a young man described how he was targeted for regular harassment all through his K–12 education without teachers once speaking up on his behalf. The man went on to say that he finally had found respect and support from peers and instructors at the university and was willing to talk about his experiences for the sake of others being discriminated against. Such anecdotes provide examples and support to students who might otherwise feel marginalized.

(dis)Ability

More and more, students with differing needs have become a part of today's college classrooms. Many different terms have been used with these students, including, disability, ableness, exceptional, challenged, and special needs. The irony is that we are all different and unique in many ways and along many dimensions. Having a label itself is not the issue. It is what it signifies in the minds of others that is often a negative connotation (Heward, 2009). Inclusive college instructors need to carefully consider their students as individuals with strengths and areas for growth, instead of viewing them in a one-dimensional fashion and comparing them to other students.

College students with declared disabilities should notify their college instructors of their needs in writing. Their college instructors are then obligated by federal and state laws to follow all required accommodations indicated by the campus office in charge of student disabilities. This can be anything from more time taking tests, arranging for note takers, or by providing copies of Power Point presentations. College instructors can be held accountable for fulfilling these legal rights, but inclusive college instructors will look for other ways to help their students become valued members of the learning community.

Students with physical disabilities have benefited from legislation requiring accommodations such as ramp access to buildings, but more subtle barriers can still be present. Outside doors have push buttons for automatic openings, but in one example, the inside classroom door was so heavy that a student in her wheelchair could not open the door alone. At the beginning of class and at mid-break, the instructor posted different students at the door to assist. This simple adjustment to the class may have prevented additional problems from occurring. Classroom arrangements such as fixed tables might restrict the mobility of students in wheelchairs, but inclusive college instructors can plan group activities with this in mind, having other students switch places.

Regionality and Nationality

The student population in state universities still tends to be dominated by those who grew up and live in near-by communities. Students from other states may feel self-conscious because of different accents and perspectives, but cultural conflicts based on region are usually minor and can generally be handled by the students themselves. Almost every campus has seen an influx of international students, particularly at the graduate level. Asian students have been a significant part of the university population for years, but now students are coming from areas which previously restricted large numbers from living abroad, the biggest example being the Republic of China. Students from the former Soviet Republic are also more likely to be present. Although each national and cultural group offers its own challenge, in common these groups of students tend to be well prepared academically and highly motivated. They often struggle with academic English, however, and make consistent grammatical mistakes, such as incorrect usage of the articles "a" and "the" (not found in Asian languages). Moreover, many international students come from cultures that demand total respect of and obedience to teachers by students. For them, speaking up in class and challenging anyone's viewpoint is inappropriate and rude.

Inclusive college instructors can encourage students to contribute by making sure they are not forced to contribute until they are settled and at ease in the classroom. The combination of their limited fluency in English and discomfort with the casual give-and-take of American university classrooms might initially paralyze international students. Inclusive college instructors can facilitate their classroom participation by choosing questions that fit the students' knowledge and level of English. For these students especially, avoiding loss of face or embarrassment in front of classmates is essential. Cooperative learning groups also can help because the students can take leadership roles in the small-group discussions without as much risk of failure. Reminding all students to be supportive of each other and to give each other time to contribute to discussions is an important key to success.

CULTURAL LEARNING AND COMMUNICATION STYLES

Cultural groups can also influence how individuals think and behave in learning situations. Although individuals within groups can vary greatly according to their own backgrounds and experiences, cultural groups on the whole might show certain patterns of thinking and behaving. For instance, Southeast Asian cultures have long histories of oral storytelling, so students from those cultures might relate information in a more circular, scene-setting way than American instructors expect. Stereotyping individuals is not helpful, but some generalization is necessary to understand what is happening in confusing situations. Being aware of different possibilities in learning and communication styles is vital.

The mainstream culture in the United States encourages individual achievement and competition among peers. In other cultures, competition is frowned upon and cooperation is expected. A good compromise is for inclusive instructors to have some assignments that require individual work and some that require student collaboration. In-class use of small groups also gives more students chances to participate. With large classes of students, small groups are harder to manage, but they still can be used effectively for brainstorming and quick discussions.

Cultural time preferences can be seen in classrooms in various forms, from students regularly arriving late or being late with assignments to spontaneous conversations. For *polychromic cultures*, time is more elastic. Appointment schedules are not as important and events are not always sequenced but might be overlapping. Conversations might involve individuals talking at the same time and actively responding to the topic rather than waiting for a turn to speak. Younger students, brought up in a world of multi-media, tolerate background noise and often study with music or television going. Inclusive instructors can balance their need for quiet attentiveness during mini-lecture times with student need for simultaneous verbal participation during small group sessions.

Cultural communication styles can affect the verbal and non-verbal communication in classrooms. American college instructors often have a fast-patterned lecture and recitation style. This style suits students who have a very fast response time, usually European American men, according to Mary Budd Rowe's (1969) research on wait time, starting 40 years ago and continuing through the decades. She found that white women and students of color on the whole took longer to respond, but if instructors waited at least three to five seconds after asking a question, these students also contributed to the classroom discussions. For students with English as a second language, an even longer amount of wait time is usually necessary for them to compose an answer. Responding to questioning itself can be embarrassing to many students, particularly those students whose cultures put an importance on not losing face or being embarrassed in front of others.

Different cultural communication styles can also be seen in situations such as when college instructors become impatient with students' seemingly roundabout way of answering a question. "Get to the point" might be what college instructors are thinking while the students are deliberately setting the scene for the requested information. The instructors' *low-context* cultural influences require that answers to be direct and without extra details from the context. The students' *high-context* cultural influences require that answers be complete with the richness of details. Learning to follow a step-by-step process to arrive at a conclusion can be a very difficult task for some students, especially international graduate students who have never experienced this kind of thinking and writing in their undergraduate years.

Relationship building is a difficult task for inclusive college instructors, particularly those who have large classes of students. With a diverse population of students, inclusive instructors also need to be conscious of how they interact with individuals. Attempting to learn all the names of students is a good start. In many institutions, class lists with photographs can be printed out and used as prompts. Some informality between instructors and students is typical in American classrooms, but too much might be offensive to cultures with traditional respect for teachers and to older students. Similarly, revealing personal experiences can help students gain insight, but professional boundaries must be honored. In any case, showing respect of students and enjoyment of the teaching role and subject content can help to establish comfortable learning communities in classrooms.

CONCLUSIONS

Cultural issues can be very subtle and what looks like a common sense approach to one group can be seen as discriminatory to another. Racial, class, gender, religious, and other cultural groups have different world views on many aspects of life such as work habits, time, personal space, or saving face. Although inclusive college instructors cannot expect to recognize, honor, and use all cultural differences in the classroom, they can make a sincere effort to appreciate other cultural perspectives, recognize cultural mismatches, and negotiate cultural clashes when they occur.

Inclusive college instructors have the three-fold challenging yet rewarding responsibility of:

1. learning about their own cultural influences and personal ways of teaching and learning;
2. learning about their students' cultural influences and ways of learning; and
3. applying what has been learned to the classroom curriculum, instruction, and assessment.

Most important of all, inclusive college instructors have the responsibility of setting the tone for the classroom environment, one where learning takes place in a risk-free context, one where students willingly participate as individuals or groups in the process of teaching and learning. As classroom teachers, inclusive college instructors must also be learners, demonstrating that in this information age world, no one person could possibly have all or even the majority of knowledge about any one subject. Collaborative efforts are needed for complex learning to take place, and all students need to contribute to the quality of each course. With such a diverse student population in the classrooms, students must help each other and the instructors so that all students can be successful. All viewpoints are not only wanted, but also needed for deep understanding of course content.

REFERENCES

American Association for University Women (AAUW). (1992). *How schools short-change girls.* Washington, DC: American Association for University Women.

American Association of University Women (AAUW). (1998). *Gender gaps: Where schools still fail our children.* Washington, DC: American Association for University Women.

Brown, S. C., & Kysilka, M. L. (2002). *Applying multicultural and global concepts in the classroom and beyond.* Boston, MA: Allyn & Bacon.

Brown, S. C., Mir, C., & Warner, M. (1996). Improving teacher practice utilizing curriculum theory: A conversation with William Schubert. *The Educational Forum, 60*(4), 348–359.

Gay, G. (1994). A synthesis of scholarship in multicultural education. Retrieved on February 13, 2009, from www.ncrel.org/sdrs/areas/issues/educatrs/leadrshp/le0gay.htm

Heward, W. L. (2009). *Exceptional children: An introduction to special education* (9th ed). Upper Saddle River, NJ: Pearson Education, Inc.

Howard, G. (1999). *We can't teach what we don't know: White teachers, multicultural schools.* New York: Teachers College Press.

Lyons, R. E., McIntosh, M., Kysilka, M. L. (2003). *Teaching college in an age of accountability.* Boston: Allyn & Bacon.

Rowe, M. B. (1969). Science, silence, and sanctions. *Science and Children, 6*(6). 11–13.

Sadker, M. & Sadker, D. (1994). *Failing at fairness: How our schools cheat girls.* New York: Simon & Schuster.

Sleeter, C. E., & McLaren, P. L. (1995). Introduction: Exploring connections to build a critical multiculturalism. In C. E. Sleeter & P. L. McLaren (Eds.), *Multicultural education, critical pedagogy, and the politics of difference* (pp. 5–32). Albany, NY: State University of New York.

Zimpher, N. L. (1989). The RATE project: A profile of teacher education students. *Journal of Teacher Education, 40*(6), 27–30.

CHAPTER 3

WHEN READING IN COLLEGE IS A PROBLEM

What Really Matters?

Alexander B. Casareno

KEY TERMS

Active Reading; Critical and Analytical Reading; Elaborated Instruction/ Elaborated Interrogation; Practice at Reading; Prior Knowledge; Reading Strategies/Strategic Reading

REFLECTIVE QUESTIONS

- Why is it that certain college students can succeed in learning the content of their college courses when other students cannot succeed?
- What does the inclusive college instructor need to understand about learners and learning so as to allow diverse students to be successful?
- What reading strategies will work to allow students to be successful?

Teaching Inclusively in Higher Education, pages 39–57
Copyright © 2010 by Information Age Publishing

INTRODUCTION

Reading in college goes beyond decoding or announcing words. Reading in college necessarily entails the reader to interpret, to analyze, to synthesize and to evaluate all that is read so as to build a new knowledge base—a personal knowledge base—that will be informed by what one has read, together with the knowledge informed in other ways (e.g. knowledge gained through lecture or lab classes). The skills of interpretation, analysis, synthesis, and evaluation are skills that are needed throughout the college and university curriculum and these skills need to be taught, to be reinforced, to be modeled, and most importantly, to be woven into instruction in such a way that they become as important for a college and university reader as decoding text is to a beginning reader.

To develop the point that reading goes beyond decoding and to identify contexts where college and university professors can facilitate students to read critically and analytically (i.e., to think critically and analytically about what they read and as they read), this chapter will use examples of how college level text can be and should be taught with the use of reading strategies. Because it is the goal of this chapter to help inclusive college instructors develop a theory and practice for teaching reading as they teach content (any content, whether that content is literature, sociology, chemistry, or finance), this first section of the chapter will ground the strategies offered into a theory of practice that is informed through reading research and research on learning. In the section that follows, a series of organizing principles and instructional strategies will be offered. The purpose of these organizing principles and instructional strategies will help to provide the reader with a framework for college-level reading instruction that will allow inclusive college instructors to create opportunities of success for a wide diversity of learners in the classroom. The chapter contains examples of how reading can be infused across the college curriculum with the goal being that of allowing all learners to succeed with college reading demands so as to be more successful with their learning, showing what is possible by telling the stories of others who struggle with the demands of reading in college.

WHEN READING IN COLLEGE IS A PROBLEM

Deanna is a 19-year-old learner attending community college. Diagnosed with a reading disability back in high school, Deanna entered community college with accommodations for her disability from the Disability Programs and Services office. Because of a previously-diagnosed disability, Deanna was entitled to full accommodations for her classes in college. Partly because of her reading disability and partly because Deanna scored so very low on the reading/language assessment test all incoming students take, Deanna was placed in a Basic Reading Skills course, a course two levels below college level reading. The expected reading level in this course is 6th to 9th grade reading. Accommodations to assist in the learning process for Deanna included note-taking services in the classroom, extended time on tests, a scribe for written tests, test proctoring outside of the classroom, audio-recording of lectures, and preferential seating in the classroom. Aside from preferential seating near the instructor or near the overhead projector and white board, Deanna opted to use all of the available accommodations.

The semester ended for Deanna much as it began: struggling to understand that reading is more than decoding words on a page. According to Deanna's instructor, the problem was not that Deanna did not try to comprehend what she was reading, and not that she couldn't comprehend much of what she was reading with instruction and with accommodations in her instruction, but the reality was that Deanna didn't know how to comprehend and didn't understand why she needed to comprehend when reading. As she once explained out of frustration, "I have difficulty with the main idea. It's hard and I don't know why I have to find it. Why can't the author just tell me what I'm supposed to know?"

On the surface such a statement about the main idea isn't necessarily indicative of a reader with problems because in college English composition classes, (as well as high school English classes), English instructors spend a great deal of time telling students to make themselves clear. English instructors also spend a great deal of time teaching students to write the main idea sentences and thesis statements when essay writing. From that perspective, Deanna's statement may well be representative of what she was taught and what she has learned: good writers are clear and good writers write clear thesis statements that tell the reader what to expect. Of course this advice, as good as it may be, ignores the fact that a great deal of "good" writing will start from an unstated main idea. In fact, entire genres of writing don't even have or call for stated main ideas. Deanna's problem identifying main ideas and thesis statements didn't just stem from genres where main ideas were not present or from writing where the reader could infer the main idea. Deanna couldn't break down an essay even if the main idea was stated this way: "The purpose of this chapter is to...," or "The main idea of this paragraph is . . .," or "The thesis presented in this paper argues. . ."

Reading in college is a problem when the reading demands do not match what the learner can do. As college is a place where reading demands will by nature increase and will by nature probably surpass much of what learners can do in reading, it obviously behooves inclusive college instructors who expect their students to read to be able to allow their students to be successful when reading. The purpose of this chapter is to identify contexts where inclusive college instructors can facilitate success by introducing reading strategies were appropriate and required. Open access colleges such as community colleges cannot necessarily expect *all* students to know how to read well enough to succeed within all curricula, but even at the graduate school level inclusive college instructors may find that many of the same problems community college students exhibit in reading also exist there.

LOOKING AT WHAT MATTERS FOR DIVERSE READERS IN COLLEGE READING

As a graduate student in elementary education at a private liberal arts college in the Pacific Northwest, Kati enrolled in an elementary school curriculum and instruction course. In graduate courses, it was expected that Kati and her classmates could read and that these students could be expected to handle graduate-level reading, but such an assumption did not always turn out to be the case for Kati.

Yes, Kati could read and she could even use strategies to read, but her difficulty came in understanding that what she was reading she was expected to use critically. This was the same problem that Deanna had. When Deanna verbalized that she wanted the author to tell her exactly what the text meant, Deanna meant she didn't want to have to think about the text any more than to read it. Deanna could comprehend the text to understand the main idea if she used the strategies taught her; she could even make other appropriate inferences about the text if she tried and was guided to do so in a well-structured lesson on inferences or drawing conclusions, but the bottom line is that Deanna didn't want to try to read in between the lines. Neither did Kati. Obviously as a graduate student and a successful undergraduate at a prestigious liberal arts college in the middle-West, Kati could read better than Deanna. She had successfully managed to navigate through university in an English literature program and she had been admitted to a graduate teacher education program, but like Deanna, Kati didn't want to read beyond the text. It was easier to take the low road and only understand at the level of literal comprehension.

In the 21st century, American colleges and universities are very diverse institutions. American community colleges began in a time and context when education for the masses of a particular community was valued (Vaughn, 2006). Part and parcel to the expansion of the community college was the concept of open admissions whereby virtually all those wishing to go to college could go as long as they could get there (Vaughn, 2006). One can argue that a result of an open door policy in college admission has been the arrival of students who do not have the basic skills necessary for college study and success. However, open enrollment does not explain the totality of students who may experience reading difficulty in college and university.

As shown above, even graduate students can experience difficulty reading when the expectations of the reader do not match the expectations of the instructor or the demands of the course or the text. Similarly, college students without appropriate reading strategies, or students who enter with ill-defined skills, will experience difficulty reading when it is expected that students will be ready to learn from the texts presented and required.

Given the fact that students in colleges can and will experience difficulty in reading, what does the inclusive college instructor need to understand about learners and learning so as to allow diverse students to be successful? What reading strategies will work to allow students to be successful? To answer these questions, an understanding of how curriculum and instruction can be designed to support students so they learn the content will provide the reader with a theory and practice of how reading can be part of the college experience for the inclusive college instructor and the student.

PURPOSE AND MEANING IN LEARNING

Learning in academic contexts can occur when connections are made with the *prior knowledge* of the learner and the added new knowledge by the instructor (Pugh, Pawan, & Antommarchi, 2000). Vygotsky (1978) postulates that learning occurs in small contexts. According to Vygotsky, learning occurs incrementally as learners make connections between what they know and what they are being taught. The space between these two extremes is, as Vygotsky terms it, the *Zone of Proximal Development* (ZPD). From this perspective, Hogan and Pressley (1997) conclude students can learn new knowledge when their prior knowledge is recognized, validated, and perhaps even related to the new knowledge of the professor or of the text.

Prior knowledge of students can take many forms (Pugh, Pawan, & Antommarchi, 2000) and college instructors may not know what the students know. One inclusive chemistry instructor has found that by asking them to write about their goals and their life histories that have led them to college and to his class, he can find themes to address in his lectures as needed. Such themes might be how chemistry relates to pharmaceutical medications, how chemistry relates to non-pharmaceutical drugs, how chemistry relates to the food we eat, how chemistry relates to the onset of Type II Diabetes.

College and university students also hold prior knowledge about reading including how to read, why to read, and when to read (Pugh, Pawan, & Antommarchi. 2000). Braunger and Lewis's (1998) work on understanding what is important to know about how students develop strong reading skills suggests that when instructors can connect to the literacy skills of learners, more and greater success in reading can occur. Beyond success in academic reading, Algood, Risko, Alvarez, and Fairbanks (2000) argue that experiencing pleasure in reading occurs when instructors connect students to the literacy demands of texts, i.e., students have a reason to read and can find pleasure in doing so.

In asking students to write about their goals and their life histories, inclusive instructors can essentially learn how these students use literacy to express themselves and how they view literacy. Undoubtedly students may write about hating to read. In order for students to engage with the textbooks, college instructors must somehow give them a purpose and meaning for reading about the content. This may be easy enough if the textbook provides students with purpose: learning objectives that are stated at the beginning of the chapters and vocabulary is introduced often with definitions and examples (See Ch. 4 for additional information). Some college instructors have traditionally just assigned chapters to read per each week of the term. Inclusive college instructors specifically tell students which chapters to read and which learning objectives or vocabulary are critical. Students do better with content in classroom discussions when they have at least read what instructors expect they read. Inclusive college instructors understand now that learning of content just does not happen by osmosis, but it is learned by students and it is taught by instructors. By teaching the students what is important to understand about the topic, the students can read the textbook and relate that material to class discussions. By directing students what to read, inclusive college instructors provide students a scaffold to another level of learning that occurs in classroom discussions; learning occurs incrementally as students strive to make sense of what they have read and what they are discussing about the topics at hand (see for example, Hogan & Pressley, 1997).

USING PRIOR KNOWLEDGE TO MOVE BEYOND PRIOR KNOWLEDGE

College and university students enter the classroom with a variety of prior knowledge that can either hinder or allow for success in learning. Prior knowledge in how to do college, how to study, how to ask questions, how to speak to instructors, how to write essays, and, of course, how to read are all knowledge bases that can help one to learn (Nist & Holschuh, 2000). Similarly, all this prior knowledge can also impinge upon students' progress if the prior knowledge is not fully developed or if the students access the wrong prior knowledge at a certain time, or if students are unable to adjust their prior knowledge to help them understand what a specific college course or task requires (Algood, Risko, Alvarez, & Fairbanks, 2000). For the inclusive college instructor who wants students to be able to use prior knowledge to allow them to learn, and as learning theory acknowledges the role of prior learning to new learning, it is important to understand just how to have students access and use the prior knowledge they may possess about a certain content area (Bransford, 1985), and the prior knowledge they may possess about reading and about studying. By using this type of knowledge, students will be able to use prior knowledge towards successful learning (Algood, Risko, Alvarez, & Fairbanks, 2000).

One example may illustrate the point. After a few years in college full-time, Foster needed to pass a course that he had failed twice before. Although he already had some prior knowledge, the text would still be difficult to get through for him even when applying reading strategies to his learning. Instruction began in critical reading strategies with assistance from the Reading and Writing Lab designed to help Foster learn more effectively from his history textbook. By the third week of the semester, Foster's prior knowledge no longer could help him. While he could put together a summary if he had background on the topic, he couldn't put together a summary if he hadn't read the chapter.

While he continued to visit the Reading and Writing Lab and continued to receive instruction in how to read strategically (e.g., he was taught how to locate main ideas, how to determine paragraph/text structure to help identify key learning propositions), Foster persisted in actually not reading. When confronted as to why he was not completing assigned chapters or why he had not completed assigned homework, Foster used a variety of reasons to explain his failings (i.e., his wife was divorcing him, he had to take a long bus ride to campus disallowing him focused time to read, the demands of other courses). Not once did Foster ever communicate that he was not reading in the history course because of the difficulty with history or with reading. When asked why he would use a strategy that proved to not be that helpful in learning the content, Foster indicated that the reading strategies he had been taught were just too time consuming. Motivation matters and while Foster agreed, he continued to explain away his behavior. By week six, it was obvious that Foster was again failing history. The midterm was scheduled, but Foster never showed. His attendance in the history course after that became very sporadic.

Foster's story is unique because while he does have prior knowledge that should allow him to be successful, he is not. He also has prior knowledge of how to think critically within the course because he has experienced such contexts before in his previous sojourns through the course and in other college courses. However, Foster's prior knowledge is limited not because he failed the course two times, but because he only gained a limited knowledge of the content and a limited knowledge of how critical thinking was taught or expected in the course. While college students may enter classrooms with the motivation to learn, motivation may not be enough

(Algood, Risko, Alvarez, & Fairbanks, 2000). While learners may be able to discern particular purposes for learning, having purpose for learning may not be enough. While students may possess all types of prior knowledge to assist them in learning, prior knowledge may not be enough to allow a particular learner to be successful in a particular college course when it comes to learning new knowledge.

Instruction that allows for success in the college curricula would recognize the need for the inclusive college instructor to instill motivation that directs students to learn, makes clear the purpose of learning beyond the need to learn, and allow the prior knowledge of students to inform the present learning (Algood, Risko, Alvarez, & Fairbanks, 2000; Nist & Holschuh, 2000). Since accessing prior knowledge is paramount to new learning, students must be able to use prior knowledge in such a way as to learn. Inclusive college instructors should therefore look for opportunities to help students focus their prior knowledge and use organizing principles for strategic reading, so that new learning can occur.

ORGANIZING PRINCIPLES FOR STRATEGIC READING

Reading in college requires students to think deeply about what they read. Whether students are reading in biology, mathematics, welding, cosmetology, sociology, or English, the point of textbooks is to teach students something they do not know, or perhaps to present students with a knowledge base necessary to understanding the discipline. However, the information learned from textbooks is what college instructors use to help students think about the subject being studied. The deeper a student reads the text, the more successful the student will be in connecting with the topic and succeeding in the discipline. Reading deeply is *critical and analytical reading* (Adler & Van Doren, 1972). To read critically is to question what one is reading. According to Adler and Van Doren (1972, pp. 46–7), a critical reader approaches the reading task by asking questions such as "Why am I reading this? How will this text help me to understand the learning goals of the course? What do I need to know to learn the material and what do I need to know that will help me make the deep connections required by the discipline?" The following example of Max illustrates how a college student can develop into a critical reader in the context of instruction with an inclusive college instructor.

Using Critical and Analytical Reading Principles

The Analytical Reading course began with a novel study of *The Portrait of Dorian Gray* (Wilde, 1898). That novel opens with Wilde's statement that "There is no such thing as a moral or an immoral book. Books are well written, or badly written. That is all." The college instructor challenged the students to determine for themselves whether the story was a moral one or if simply the story was either well written or badly written. As the class discussed the first chapter of Dorian Gray, Max related it to the devotion of Siddhartha's (Hesse, 1999) best friend as similar to Basil's devotion to Dorian. As other students had no idea what Siddhartha was about, Max encouraged everybody to read the novel and then got quiet. After class, Max admitted that while he remembered parts of the story, he couldn't really understand most on his own. The college instructor challenged Max to first focus on the novel he had to read for class and then to think about how Siddhartha's personal story might be similar to and different from Dorian's personal story. Within a week, Max had read both books and was leading class discussions on what he saw as Dorian's spiritual path. More importantly, Max related Dorian's story and Siddhartha's story to his own story of learning the importance of reading.

Analytical reading is the process of connecting what one reads with prior knowledge and learned knowledge. This occurs as the reader is questioning prior to reading, during reading, and after reading. The analytical reader actively searches for the answers to pre-reading questions and actively makes connections to questions that arise during reading and after reading. Analytical readers not only want to know what they are reading and why, they also want to know how what they are reading connects to what they have learned previously, what they are learning at present, and to whatever else they will read or have read. Analytical readers make connections not only to the topic being read but also to other topics even when such connections are not explicit. Max had not only experienced success at analytical reading, but he had also come to understand the veracity behind Wilde's statement of a book being neither moral nor immoral. As Max explained in his final critique on the novel, "A well-written story is one where everything works in the end. The plot, no matter how predicable, works when, in the end, everything is tied together and you understand the characters of the novel. That is why I like Dorian Gray."

While many students have some knowledge of the course content, that knowledge may be limited when it comes to advanced study in most any field. Knowing that students come with limited prior knowledge of content, inclusive college instructors can access that content by using a KWL chart that capitalizes upon what students know and challenges them to extend their learning so that they can learn more. Instructors may start units of study with a KWL chart. For example, when discussing the revolutionary war, they may start with the question: "What do you know about the American Revolution?" After students have brainstormed all that they know, the next question posed to the students on the KWL chart is "What do you *want* to know about the American Revolution?" or "What will be on the test?"

As students study the chapters in the assigned texts, they will be able to fill in this column of the chart. This column could also be enhanced by class lecture. Finally, as students review the unit and perhaps prepare for the test, or as they prepare to understand the importance of the revolutionary war upon the development of Northern and Southern states, they will complete the final column of the chart: "What have you *learned* about the American Revolution that is new? Or, what have you learned that may explain the development of two distinct regions of the nation: the North and the South?" (See example in Table 3.1).

Using Elaborated Integration Principles

Elaboration in instruction can be defined as the strategy of asking students to be explicit and elaborate in identifying what they know so they can learn something new (Casareno, 2002). *Elaborated integration* is the strategy of asking "why" as students read text to learn (Nist & Holschuh, 2000). In teaching students to analyze non-fiction texts, such as when reading for the purpose of research, the inclusive college instructor should first direct students to find the author's key ideas that lead to the central argument of the text. Once students identify the argument and the key support for the argument, the instructor may ask students to make the author's ideas neutral. Using the concept of syntopical reading, or the idea of learning how to read and understand across a variety of texts on a topic, from Adler and Van Doren (1972), the students can be guided to make key ideas of an argument neutral by asking *who, what, when, where, why, how* questions about the propositions. Those *who, what, when, where, why, how* questions then allow the student to determine whether the author has sufficient support for the argument.

TABLE 3.1.   Example of a KWL Chart in a History Course

What do you *know* about the American Revolution	What do you need to know and *want* to know about the American Revolution? (What will be on the test?)	What have you *learned* about the American Revolution that is new?
Started in 1776	Why did the people in the colonies want to be independent?	The desire for independence had a lot to do with the feeling of being over-taxed
Years before the war, colonists were unhappy with British rule and taxation.	Was independence the original goal?	For some independence was the goal; for others the goal was to make King George know that the colonies needed to be treated fairly.

As research in college demands that students not report back what they have read, but rather to interpret, synthesize, and evaluate what they have read so as to build new knowledge on a specific topic, making propositions neutral becomes key in analyzing text. The example in Table 3.2 demonstrates how the inclusive college instructor can ask students to explain the neutrality of two short essays that might be used to answer the researchable question (i.e., a question that can be researched) of "What roles does television have on children's behaviors?"

After students ask questions to explore the neutrality of the author's claims, they reflect back upon what they have read to determine if the author has indeed backed up her or his argument or whether the argument and the various propositions put forth to support the argument are valid

TABLE 3.2. Example of Elaborated Interrogation of Texts When Learning to Read for the Purpose of Research

General Questions to Make Propositions Neutral	Violence on Television (APA, 2000)	Hate Violence? Turn it Off! (Goodman, 2000)
	(Major Claim:"Violence on television leads to aggressive behavior in children and Teens")	(Major claim: Parents are the one responsible for any effect of violent television shows on their children.)
Who?	Who is the demographic studied to come to this conclusion?	Who is having the problem with violent TV shows?
What?	What did the research look at? What did it find exactly? What exactly are children and teens doing after being exposed to violent TV shows?	What can society or parents to do curb any possible negative effects of violence upon TV upon children and teens?
When?	When does this aggressiveness show up?	When is violence on TV a problem? Has the problem gotten worse with the advent of TV that is available 24/7/365?
Where?	Where are children and teens being aggressive? Is there a difference in behavior at home and at school?	Where is the problem arising?
Why?	Why are children and teens led to aggressive behavior from watching violent TV shows when adults may not be so led?	Why do violent TV shows persist if they are so bad for children and teens?
How?	How was the study completed?	How can the potential negative effects of violence on TV for children and teens be alleviated?

or logical. By elaborating upon what the students already know of the text from a first reading, the strategy of interrogating the text allows students to analyze whether or not a particular claim is valid. Students also come to understand that reading for research does require them to dig deeper into what they read so they can move beyond the reporting stage when it comes to writing the research paper.

Using active reading principles

In any college or university classroom there will be a wide variety of readers. While some students will enjoy reading and studying, others will read only to learn what is required, and still others will avoid reading as much as possible even if they purchase the required texts. When looking beyond who is and who is not reading, what should become apparent to inclusive college instructors is that those who truly understand the importance of reading in college will be the most successful students in the class. They are successful because not only can they read critically, but they can also read actively.

Active reading is to take control of reading (Adler & Van Doren, 1972). Active readers understand that as they read they are doing so with a purpose in mind. Active readers search for answers to questions and even question what they are reading. Active readers look for key terms and guiding questions to textbooks and they scan the introduction, conclusions and even the chapter test to learn what they must learn and know of the content they are taught (Adler & Van Doren, 1972). As active readers read and internalize what they are learning from text, they anticipate what will come next and they read to verify their predictions. Not only do active readers purposefully interpret what is on the page, they also evaluate what is on the page. They decide if what they are reading is going to be useful to their learning goals and they adjust their goals as they read and learn more. In their classic text on intelligent reading, Adler and Van Doren (1972) summarize active reading as the process of questioning what one reads. The specific questions an active reader asks vary by genre, but ultimately if the goal is to make meaning from text, the questions to ask are these:

1. What is the text about?
2. Why details are important to understanding the overall text?
3. How is the text believable as presented?
4. How and why is the text (or argument or story behind the text) significant? (Adler & Van Doren, 1972, pp. 46–47)

As most inclusive college instructors are good readers, they also are active readers. Thus, it may not seem out of place for inclusive college instructors to expect that their students would read actively, but expecting students to behave in certain ways is not always to be the case. When a reader approaches any text and asks "What am I reading?" that reader approaches the task differently than the student who just opens a textbook (any textbook in any discipline) and starts reading. While many textbooks in college are designed to help students learn the important content, inclusive college instructors continually will encounter students who will open their textbooks, which are hundreds and hundreds of pages long, and start reading from the beginning to the end with very little understanding of what they are doing other than reading an assigned section.

Inclusive college instructors may well first teach students the importance of previewing a chapter to learn the important vocabulary, key ideas of the chapter, and the objectives of the chapter and to determine what really is important to understand in the chapter by reading the section summaries and conclusion of the chapter (See Ch. 4 for additional information). In this manner inclusive college instructors will find that if students are to really take charge of their reading or they need to become active readers. Thus, college students should be directed to approach any text (fiction or non-fiction) they might read for any college class, with the intent of:

a.   questioning what the text is about;
b.   determining what important details need to be known to understand the main idea, the argument or the story's theme;
c.   analyzing the truth or believability behind the central argument or the story's theme; and
d.   interpreting the significance of the argument or the story by looking at how the argument is developed and presented or how the story is told (Adler & Van Doren, 1972, pp. 46–47).

Using the Principle of Practice

While college students have to complete a great deal of reading, they may do so without ever really improving their own reading skills. Improving reading skills requires *practice at reading*. Reading a lot to a college student often means a) students read and re-read chapters in textbooks b) spend hours reading everything assigned, and c) read study guides, websites, blogs, or professor's notes to better understand their required texts. While a blog or a condensed version of a text may be easier to read than a textbook or novel, students who do all of this extra reading often fail to realize that by reading a lot of new material to understand what is in the textbook, they have stumbled upon a new problem: how to synthesize all of the information they may pick up from all the other sources of reading they have chosen to do. For the college students who think reading is about memorizing what is in the text, the task of memorizing is made that much more difficult when there is more and more text to memorize.

Rarely do college students seem to practice reading when reading all of this content. Rarely do students read all they can on a topic unless assigned a research project. Rarely do students discuss reading for pleasure or reading to learn something on their own because they are curious. In the earlier example, Max chose to read on his own beyond what was required. Max said he felt better prepared for additional graduate studies because he had learned to like to read and to question as he read. Practice makes perfect, or at least that is what experts tell novices. In colleges, instructors are experts in their content areas, and while many college instructors may become experts in their respective disciplines because they had the desire to succeed and the ability to persist through graduate programs, undoubtedly they also succeeded because they practiced. Learning to think as a scientist, a mathematician, a logician, a writer, or some other master in a certain field takes practice and time. Practice at reading evolves over time and is strategic.

Strategic reading of texts allows learners to practice their reading skills. Good strategic readers start practicing their reading before the actual act of reading: they question what will be read and why. While reading, good strategic readers search for appropriate responses to questions asked by looking into the text itself. Finally, good strategic readers practice what to learn when reviewing what has been read.

Professor Robert M. was probably one of the best inclusive college instructors this author ever had. In an Introduction to Sociology course in community college, Professor M taught students to practice reading by using the SQ3R strategy to guide reading and comprehension. SQ3R means Survey—Question—Read—Recite—Review. It allows learners to practice reading before, during and after reading. When asked to read Emile Durkheim's classic text *Suicide* (1979) as freshmen in college, the entire class was thrown. When just about every student came back to class complaining about having difficulty understanding the beginning of the book, Professor M asked everybody to survey (S) what they already knew about suicide: what is suicide, why does it happen, how does it happen, when does it happen, etc.

After discussing what students knew on the topic, Professor M directed everybody to read the editor's introduction to the text and to ask any other questions that might arise on the topic after reading that introduction (Q). After discussing these new questions about suicide, Professor M directed everybody to read the text, but he also explicitly directed students to read to find answers to questions about suicide that came out of the survey of the topic or out of reading the introduction to the book; students were challenged to discover if their own theories about suicide were correct (1st R). In class, over several occasions, students talked about what Durkheim had to say about suicide. To assess their learning, Professor M asked students recite and to discuss what they knew about suicide from the text (2nd R). Finally, all students wrote homework assignments reviewing or summarizing what was being read (3rd R). SQ3R not only helped this author to read and to comprehend a very difficult text, but it also taught the author that one could have a plan when reading. (See Table 3.3 for an explanation of the steps in SQ3R.)

Research into what distinguishes successful readers from readers with difficulties points to the fact that good readers are successful largely because they employ strategies as they read text. Reading strategically means to have a plan prior to reading, during reading and after reading. That plan can consist of asking questions before reading, taking notes during reading and reviewing after reading. Several reading strategies are available to inclusive instructors and to college learners which will allow them to be most successful with text. Strategic college readers are by definition active readers. Furthermore, reading strategies allow readers to think critically and analytically about what they read; strategic readers then are good readers because they take control of their reading.

Strategic readers understand that successful reading means they must seek to understand the text beyond what authors write. Finally, strategic readers' plans for reading mean they read for a purpose; they are successful students because they have a plan to help them learn. Asking students to discuss what they know and what to know about the texts they are required to read does allow for them to connect to the text. Likewise, encouraging students to read strategically, to read for a purpose, and to question as they read, does help the learner to engage with reading. In Max's case, the strategies taught him encouraged him to connect his current reading with a book a teacher had discussed in the past. Even Deanna connected

TABLE 3.3. Steps in SQ3R

Survey	Question	Read	Recite	Review
Instructor poses initial questions to find out what students know about suicide.	Students are directed to read the introduction to the text Suicide and come up with other questions that need to be answered through reading.	Student read the book Suicide searching for answers to the questions posed in the survey and in the question section.	Students discuss what they have learned.	Students write about what they have learned as homework assignments.

her current reading of a text to a recent viewing of a movie. The difference between the two learners is that Deanna and Max held different levels of motivation.

FINDING PLEASURE IN READING

While a requirement to read may not be the ideal motivation for learners to find pleasure in reading, it can be a start. Algood, Risko, Alvarez, and Fairbanks (2000, pp. 210–11) recommend three steps for the inclusive college instructor to encourage learners to find pleasure in learning:

1. Allow students to express their own emotions when confronted with something new. Professor M did this when he asked his students what they thought and what they knew about the topic of the text: suicide.
2. Encourage students to access their prior knowledge when learning something new. A KWL chart can be useful here. SQ3R also helps students access their own prior knowledge.
3. Instill within students a sense of knowledge and self-worth. Max wanted to understand Oscar Wilde's novel because he wanted to know if he could read it for himself.

Danielle entered this author's reading course Vocabulary Development and Reading Strategies for College with the desire to learn. This course is one level below college level and has an expected grade level of 10th–12th grade reading. Danielle also understood intuitively that in order to comprehend both non-fiction and fiction prose, she needed to be able to read to know what the authors wanted readers to know about their essays, textbooks, stories, or novels, although she wasn't always sure just how to do that. Danielle came to understand in the course that with the strategy of finding the main idea, she could determine how the main idea is developed through details, and how the details of a text can allow the reader to determine text structure, which would lead her to understand how and why the text is written as it is.

In one activity, students were asked to imagine that they had completed their college degree goal and were sitting in the sun wearing cap and gown. After reading the introduction, the students discussed what was about to come and predicted what the essay would be about. The Neil Postman's Graduation Speech (Postman, 1985) was then read aloud by the instructor as if students were hearing it for the first time at graduation. All members of the class had a copy of the text in front of them. Danielle, unlike all the other students in the course, took out a yellow marker and an ink pen and as the speech was read, she highlighted important or interesting points and she used her pen to underline one sentence. It was clearly apparent that Danielle was ready to demonstrate that she was capable of being an active reader.

Following the recitation of the speech, generally students responded positively to the content. Many students surmised that the speech would be advice for graduates, but no one was really able or willing perhaps to be more specific. The first question then asked to the class was "What was the point of this essay? Can you find a sentence that would tell you that?" Danielle offered a sentence in the text and read it aloud. In the discussion which followed, Danielle essentially identified the main idea, the details that supported the main idea, and the text structure; and all of this happened on the second day of the course. Clearly, Danielle demonstrated the promise of being not only an analytical reader, she also understood that she could read and understand better by reading strategically. Perhaps Danielle really didn't stand out from her classmates. She took notes, referred to her notes, and stayed focused because the discussion and the questions interested her. However, Danielle had a plan that helped her learn and her motivation to learn using her reading skills was obvious.

CONCLUSIONS

When asking the question "Why is it that certain college students can succeed in learning the content of their college courses when other students cannot succeed?" the responses generated necessarily lead inclusive college instructors to look at those who does succeed and those who do not succeed. In order to fully understand who do succeed and who do not succeed, inclusive college instructors must look also at how students are taught. More specifically, when it comes to succeeding within the textbooks required in college and university courses, inclusive college instructors must look at how reading may have been, or needs to be, facilitated so students can succeed.

While Deanna, Kati, and Foster may been given opportunities and strategies to allow for learning, their non-success may be attributable not only to a lack of preparedness, but also to a lack of motivation. Deanna was provided accommodations to help her through her learning difficulties, but Deanna often chose to disengage with instruction even when curriculum was geared to her level or to her interests. When asked about a book, "What was the story all about?" Deanna answered, "Why can't the author just tell me what I'm supposed to know?" While Kati must have demonstrated an ability to think, read, and write critically in her undergraduate program in English literature, in a graduate level course she often chose not to apply these skills in her work, barely passing the course. While Foster claimed that he wanted to succeed in his history course, in reality he was merely looking for a way out of the college. Clearly for Deanna, Kati, and Foster, motivation does matter—as it does for most college students if those students are to experience success in learning.

Reflecting back upon Max's and Danielle's successes in their courses, their learning can be attributed to their willingness to learn and their willingness to use strategies to help them learn. Max always had the goal and plan of becoming a pharmacist. Perhaps because of this goal, Max saw value in analyzing a story written more than a hundred years before he had ever heard of it. While his classmates might try to argue that a story so old had nothing to do with their lives, Max countered that thought by showing them how the story could relate to his own life. Danielle continues to inspire. At any point during the week, she can be found in the learning center on campus talking to peers about how she learns. Peers seek out Danielle for help in a variety of disciplines and she is more than happy to help. Help often means showing students how to learn to read their texts.

Clearly, motivation matters. Because the diversity of any college classroom may mean that inclusive college instructors in any discipline will encounter college students who are not good readers, it behooves the instructors to allow these students to experience success by providing strategies to learn the content and knowledge locked away in the textbook. With all else being equal, (i.e., if inclusive college instructors can assume that students come to college with the motivation to learn), reading instruction that is strategic and active will go a long way to allow the diverse college learner to succeed.

REFERENCES

Adler, M. J., & Van Doren, C. (1972). *How to read a book: The classic guide to intelligent reading*, (Revised and Updated Ed.). New York: Touchstone Books. (Original work published in 1940).

Algood, W. P., Risko, V. J., Alvarez, M.C., & Fairbanks, M. (2000). Factors that influence study. In Flippo, R. F. & Caverly, D. C. (Eds.). *Handbook of college reading and study strategy research* (pp. 201–220). Mahwah, NJ: Lawrence Erlbaum Associates, Inc.

Bransford, J. (1985). Schema activation and schema acquisition. In H. Singer & R. B. Ruddell (Eds.), *Theoretical models and processes of reading*, (3rd ed., pp. 385–397). Newark, DE: International Reading Association.

Braunger, J., & Lewis. J. P. (1998). *Building a knowledge base in reading*. Newark, DE: International Reading Association.

Casareno, A. (2002). An interview with Ed Ellis: Working to improve education for adolescents with learning disabilities. *Intervention in school and clinic, 42*(5), 280–284.

Durkheim, E. (1979). *Suicide: A study in sociology.* (J. Spaulding & G. Simpson, Trans. and Eds.). New York: The Free Press. (Original work published in 1897).

Hesse, H. (1999). *Siddhartha: An Indian tale.* (J. Neugroschel, Trans.). New York: Penguin. (Original work published 1922).

Hogan, K., & Pressley, M. (1997). Becoming a scaffolder of students' learning. In *Scaffolding student learning: Instructional approaches and issues.* (pp. 185–191). Cambridge, MA: Brookline.

Nist, S., & Holschuh, J. L. (2000). Comprehension strategies and the college learner. In R.F. Flippo & D.C. Caverly (Eds.), *Handbook of college reading and study strategy research* (pp. 75–104). Mahwah, NJ: Lawrence Erlbaum Associates, Inc.

Postman, N. (1985). *My graduation speech.* Retrieved from http://www.ditext.com/postman/mgs.html

Pugh, S. L., Pawan, F., & Antommarchi, C. (2000). Academic literacy and the new college learner. In R.F. Flippo & D.C. Caverly (Eds.). *Handbook of college reading and study strategy research* (pp. 25–55). Mahwah, NJ: Lawrence Erlbaum Associates, Inc.

Vaughn, G. B. (2006). *The community college story* (5th ed.). Washington, DC: Community College Press/American Association of Community Colleges.

Vygotsky, L. (1978). *Mind in society.* (M. Cole, Trans.). Cambridge, MA: Harvard University Press.

Wilde, O. (1898). *The picture of Dorian Gray,* (Oxford World Paperback Ed.). New York: Oxford University Press. (Original work published 1898).

PART II

INCLUSIVE INSTRUCTORS AS STRATEGIC LEADERS AND CO-LEARNERS

CHAPTER 4

CHANGING INSTRUCTIONAL STRATEGIES AND METHODS TO MEET THE NEEDS OF ALL LEARNERS

Moira A. Fallon

KEY TERMS

Advanced Organizers; Discovery or Inquiry Learning; Instructional Strategies; Long Term Memory; Mnemonics; Pre-teaching; Visual Organizers

REFLECTIVE QUESTIONS

- How do instructors shift their role from past practices in the teaching and learning process to meet the needs of all students in today's classrooms?
- What specific strategies should instructors use in order to better help students to process and understand the course material?
- How can the teaching and learning process at the college level be balanced to take into consideration the needs of the learners, the complexities of the learning environment, and the instructional cycle of the content material?

Teaching Inclusively in Higher Education, pages 61–75
Copyright © 2010 by Information Age Publishing
All rights of reproduction in any form reserved.

INTRODUCTION

Education is defined and identified by the process of teaching. Heward (2009) suggests that educators consider the issues of who is being taught and how the teaching occurs in their process of examining their own teaching practices. Students with learning disabilities are perhaps the most common and fastest growing group of students with special needs on campus. Processing and producing written information in traditional forms such as papers and tests can present difficulties for these students. Sometimes college instructors present the biggest difficulty to students with varying types of learning disabilities. All students will benefit from college instructors who use a wide variety of instructional strategies, which include the use of cooperative learning groups, learning styles, and multiple intelligences (refer back to Ch. 1 for additional information). Gardner's (1997) Theory of Multiple Intelligences gives inclusive college instructors other ways of engaging students in course content. From his theory, then, inclusive instructors can expect today's students with diverse backgrounds will process information in different manners.

Gardner's (1997) first two intelligences, verbal/linguistic and logical/mathematical, are the two areas traditionally assessed in U.S. schools. Students who have these abilities can use language effectively in oral and written situations and can reason in logical step-by-step ways and in quantitative, numerical ways. These students have been successful over the years in traditional educational settings because they can learn well from college instructors who require linguistic fluency, mathematical skill, and logical convergent thought and conformity. In the past and to a large degree today, these have been the students who scored well on SATs and ACTs and earned the highest student spots in higher education. They are not the only students now attending university, however, so attention needs to be paid to the other intelligences identified by Gardner.

University students might very well have other intelligences as their strengths. Often those with musical, visual/spatial, and bodily/kinesthetic abilities choose majors such as the music, visual arts, and physical education. They participate in art shows, musical recitals, and university sports. Yet these talents are not often called upon in general education courses. Inclusive college instructors can take advantage of these talents by providing activities that draw upon students' strengths. Asking students to illustrate a concept in a creative way, put the concept definition and relationships to music, or to act out the concept are easy ways to get students involved in active learning.

Students with interpersonal abilities often become the leaders, for good or bad, in classrooms. They have street smarts and know what's going on with their classmates because they easily read the emotions and feelings of others. They usually enjoy cooperative learning groups because they get along with others so well. In contrast, students with intrapersonal strengths know themselves very well. They are more introspective and do not always work well in groups. Yet they can express their inner feelings well in various creative forms such as poetry, creative writing, and drama. They are in tune with themselves. Inclusive college instructors can provide for both types of students by having a variety of activities that require either group or individual work or a combination.

Naturalist and existentialist are the last two intelligences identified by Gardner (1997). Students with naturalist abilities are sensitive to their physical environment, working with it and using it in positive ways. They recognize and relate to the plants and animals in their surroundings and can identify patterns in the living world around them. Students with existentialist strengths question the meaning of life. They want to explore the complexities of being human and being a part of the universe. Inclusive college instructors can expect these students to see the whole picture, the patterns and theories behind the factual information. Their insights can lead other students into more in-depth understanding of the course content. They can be encouraged to present other perspectives, even doing informal research beyond class requirements. One such student got caught up in the debate between quantitative and qualitative research, investigated several qualitative studies, and asked that his findings be accepted as an alternative to a short essay assignment. These students, however, often need extra help and encouragement with organizing their notes or sequencing in-class activities.

USING INSTRUCTIONAL STRATEGIES

How to teach and reach all the college students today is the art of teaching and involves the use of a variety of instructional methods and materials. The process of planning instruction and the instructional delivery must change from past practices in order to meet the needs of all learners today. Inclusive college instructors can play an important role in supporting these students and more likely ensuring their success. The remainder of the chapter will focus on the how in using effective, research-based instructional methods and strategies that meet the needs of all students. *Instructional strategies* are the techniques, principles, or routines that help a student to acquire, process, retain, and retrieve critical information (Deschler & Schumaker, 1986). These instructional strategies have been developed for use with a variety of learners and are generally effective when used as directed. However, even when instructors develop user-friendly lectures in their teaching practices, the students must still develop study skills and their own practices to process and retain their learning. Balancing this teaching and learning process is the job of inclusive college instructors.

The main role of the inclusive college instructor is to know appropriate instructional strategies and to carefully select them for use in the course content. The selection must be based on the individual needs of the learners and match the content being taught. Once selected, there are three stages to implementing effective, research-based instructional strategies into the curricular content. The first stage is the need of the inclusive college instructor to assess prior knowledge and, based on that assessment, to pre-teach critical vocabulary. The inclusive college instructor should help students by previewing the key concepts and to organize the information so that students understand what is important from the less important concepts. The next stage is the ability to communicate the key concepts to students using a variety of instructional strategies so that they are able to process and understand the information necessary to the learning process. The final stage is the ability of the students to retrieve the information so as to apply their skills and demonstrate their understanding of the materials. Each stage of the teaching and learning process requires instructional strategies that help the students to understand the material.

PREPARING STUDENTS FOR THE LEARNING PROCESS

In the past, college instructors would have paid little attention to preparing students for content learning. This was deemed to be the job of the students themselves. The goal of college instructors is to teach their students the curricular content or the concepts, materials, and key understandings of the course. An essential part of teaching and learning is to help students understand what is being presented and the importance of that curricular content. This portion of the teaching and learning process is most often overlooked by college instructors. It is essential that instructors begin to understand the need for the process of cueing the students to what is coming, before teaching the critical content and reviewing what has been learned. For many students in K–12 classrooms, No Child Left Behind mandated students' rights to the access of core content of the curriculum. With those students now in college classrooms, this means being able to access the critical content of the discipline. Rather than jumping directly into the lecture or activity, inclusive college instructors should prepare or preview the critical concepts and vocabulary about to be taught.

Prior knowledge is a critical component of pre-teaching academic concepts. Knowing what the students in a college classroom already know helps inclusive instructors to focus their teaching in order to promote the understanding of all the students. Prior knowledge is the knowledge and understanding of words and concepts already known by the students. Assessing prior knowledge can be a valuable aid for inclusive college instructors in determining where to start teaching the vocabulary, a critical concept, and how to frame understanding of the concept. Understanding the students' prior knowledge will help the students to comprehend, and retain the information by linking the new information with the previously learned information. One instructional method for assessing prior knowledge is the use of a pretest on key concepts and vocabulary. Another is the use of a class discussion or small groups to ascertain what students already know about a given topic. Given this information on students' prior knowledge, inclusive college instructors can cue or prompt students in relating the new information to the previously known concepts. Using this instructional method will often correct misconceptions earlier and perhaps prevent them from occurring later.

Once the students' prior knowledge of key concepts and vocabulary is ascertained, inclusive college instructors can pre-teach key vocabulary words that are not part of prior learning or that are applied to the academic content in a new manner. Learning vocabulary and understanding the concepts behind the written words is a skill learner must develop. Therefore, for inclusive college instructors, teaching the explicit nature of the vocabulary terms and their concepts is critical to balancing the teaching learning process. Vocabulary can be oral or written or both. Inclusive instructors should have a clear vision of the vocabulary terms necessary to master the critical concepts. *Pre-teaching* vocabulary is the process of identifying if students already possess basic understanding of words and their meanings or to explicitly teach the word and the meaning as directly related to the course content. Pre-teaching vocabulary allows the students to prepare for more effective reading with greater understanding. A number of instructional strategies (Vaughn & Bos, 2009) can be used to introduce the vocabulary terms and to identify if the word is already part of the students' vocabulary:

- Teach the vocabulary in purposeful context.
- Teach students to both understand the term and to produce it.
- Give students the words along with their definitions, and use the terms appropriately within the curricular content.
- Match words with the key concepts, using picture, diagrams, or visual aids. Students can even draw illustrations of the words and their meaning.
- Use teacher modeling of the terms while asking students to reproduce them in their own words.
- Use an open-ended assessment tool that asks students if they have heard the words before or can project what the meaning may be.

Another important pre-teaching strategy is the use of advance organizers. *Advance organizers* are activities that orient the students to the materials for that day's class before reading or class presentation takes place. (Slavin, 2000). Advance organizers provide the students with an overview of the most important concepts to be presented or discussed. They are more effective when presented in advance of the lesson rather than after the fact. The advance organizers should inform students of the purpose of instruction, the main topics, and give an overall organizational structure to the upcoming lesson (Lentz, 1983). They may be in the form of a list of key word, daily agenda, or an outline of the day's lesson (see Table 4.1).

Researchers (Lentz, 1983, Slavin, 2000, Vaughn & Bos, 2009) have determined that using advance organizers improve academic performance and the quality of learning. Given this information, inclusive college instructors should incorporate the use of advanced organizers into each day's work. However, building the advanced organizers into the daily routine is necessary to effective use. Inclusive instructors should place the advance organizers in a place easily visible to all students. Students should be required to copy these organizers and use them as part of their note taking process. The advanced organizers chosen by college instructors should be major topics or concepts. Thus, they can be used in review for any test or as a list of major topics for the course. One common way is for inclusive college instructors to post the session agenda, along with the advance organizers, at the beginning of class, either on the board or as a Power Point. This gives

TABLE 4.1. Samples of Advanced Organizers

One of the easiest methods of using an advanced organizer is to identify key concepts with Roman numerals. This can then be developed by students into an outline for note taking.

    I. Causes of the Civil War

    II. Influences upon different regions of the US

    III. National events impact the concept of war

    IV. Economic differences among people

Another example of an advanced organizer is a key word organizer. This type of advanced organizer contains the key vocabulary highlighting the important concepts to be taught. Students can complete the organizer with definitions, how the word is used within the content, or summarize the terms in their own words.

    1. Conflict

    2. Main Characters

    3. Narrative

    4. Development of Plot

    5. Resolution

structure to a class period, and is especially helpful if class periods are three or four hours long with multiple activities and breaks.

ORGANIZING AND TEACHING CRITICAL CONTENT

The primary goal of inclusive teaching is for all students to learn, process, and understand the critical information being taught. The need for change in organization and teaching of content is in sharp contrast to the past due to the changing faces and needs of today's college students. Some students can take individual facts and pull them together, but many students today need whole picture, especially those students with varying cultures whose ways of learning are also different. There are a number of methods inclusive college instructors can use to help ensure understanding of critical content. These instructional methods or strategies are designed for the student to process the information into *long term memory* (LTM), rather than cramming the information or using solely short term memory or working memory. However, using LTM means the students must either attach the new information to some prior knowledge or to process the meaning of the new information appropriately.

Many students have learned to cram or hold new information in their working memory in order to take a test. Inclusive college instructors need to teach students specific strategies in order to assist them in understanding and retrieving the new information. Understanding the use of cognitive learning strategies is complex. It requires understanding of the role of brain in focusing attention, developing schemas, and using mega-cognition. For the purposes of this chapter, several instructional strategies inclusive college instructors can use that require the use of LTM and organization of new content into mega-cognition, rather than simply cramming it into working memory for shorter periods of time. Other chapters will provide additional instructional strategies, including the use of visual imagery (see Ch. 6 for additional information) and engaging a competent learner (see Ch. 5 for additional information).

One type of learning, *discovery* or *inquiry learning*, assists students in problem solving. The first American credited with inquiry and discovery is Dewey (1900). For Dewey, inquiry and discovery learning begins when the college student is confronted with a problem that engages intelligence and curiosity. This type of instructional method leads directly to LTM learning as students use their own learning experience to gain knowledge. Questioning, discovery learning, and inquiry find their roots as far back as Socrates (Fallon, Halquist, & Balzano, 2009; Fallon & Weinbeck, 2006). Schwab (1983) was another pioneer of the inquiry approach and was strongly influenced by Dewey. Schwab's philosophy embodied integrating inquiry teaching and the processing of learned skills into long term memory. Many students find that a guided approach to inquiry learning, even when applied outside of the science and math fields, encourages them to explore, to verbalize their thinking, and to apply their learning to their daily life. Gardner (1997) would concur with Dewey and Schwab that discovery or inquiry learning is essential for reaching all learners.

The ability to collaborate and to work more effectively with others is built upon teamwork, communication, and problem solving. Collaboration is knowledge of and ability to apply skills in a cooperative manner (Friend & Cook, 2007). The most critical collaboration skills required are creativity and flexibility in problem solving and active learning. Active participation in a small group using collaboration skills can enhance students' ability to remember and retain critical information. Effective collaboration skills are necessary in a variety of content areas. Collaboration skills are also commonly used in business, nursing, education, and other professional environments. Inclusive college instructors can create communities in which collaboration skills are taught and practiced. Some previous research (Cox, 2004) found evidence of increased sensitivity to others as part of the development of student communities within the college setting. Classroom participation can be developed that builds a sense of community and ownership, along with the retention of critical information.

Other adjustments to teaching content material may made by either college instructors or students to improve the learning process. Chunking curricular material is an instructional strategy that highlights the most important information and helps the students to classify the learning so as to make processing it easier. An example of a chunking strategy would be for the inclusive college instructor to ask students to write a *one sentence summary* (OSS) of the information (Angelo & Cross, 1993). In order to summarize or to paraphrase correctly, students must understand clearly the underlying concept. This forces the students to focus on the most critical details and concepts as they describe in their own words. Another example of chunking is to use Post-it notes or index cards. Students can draw or write their understanding of the critical content, but in chunks no greater than the size of the Post-it note or card. Other examples of chunking include predicting, summarizing, questioning, identifying the main idea, and paraphrasing. Each of these strategies requires the students to separate the important information from the lesser important. When asked to retrieve the critical information, it is often the chunked information students are able to bring to their minds.

Visual organizers are often used to help students gather, understand, organize, and summarize major concepts. Many visual organizers utilize chunking or summation strategies in their development of the organizer. There are many types of visual organizers, such as bubble maps, relationship charts, and comparison grids, among others. A number of textbooks incorporate the use of visual organizers and there are many books devoted to the appropriate use of this strategy of using visual organizers in the teaching and learning process. There is also software that inclusive college instructors or students can use to create visual organizers. Such software is made by Inspiration (www.inspiration.com). This type of software can be used for organizing, classifying, and for brainstorming of ideas. The software, or hand-drawn visual organizers, accomplishes the same thing; that is, to organize and prioritize the ideas as they are suggested. Other types of visual organizers are used to identify key terms, summarize definitions, compare concepts, and other instructional strategies. Two examples are found in Table 4.2. Visual organizers not only provide a visual picture that many students can easily process, but help students to read the text more accurately and fluently.

Many college students struggle with reading text fluently and effectively (refer back to Ch. 3 for additional information). Fluency is the ability to read text quickly, accurately, and with expression (Vaughn & Bos, 2009).

TABLE 4.2. Samples of Visual Organizers

Example 1 :Concept Diagram

Fossils

Characteristics:

Always Present	Sometimes Present	Never Present
remains	trapped	decaying

Example: Non Example:

Definition:

Fossils are remains or prints that have been preserved in the earth from many years ago
.

Example 2: Contrast and Comparison Grid

Travel within the United States	Travel outside of the United States
Passport is not required	Passport is required
Variety of transportation options is available	Variety of transportation options is available
Primary language used is English	Many languages are used depending on where you travel

This is the ability to read more automatically, yet without loss of the key ideas and important information. In the college classroom, this skill is essential to a successful academic performance. It is often a skill lacking in students for whom English is not their first language. However, inclusive college instructors can add instructional strategies to their repertoire that promote students' understanding, while not reading every written word of a textbook. Some instructional strategies to promote fluency include reading aloud. Inclusive college instructors can select important quotes, sayings, or paragraphs that underlie critical concepts. By reading aloud and dissecting or analyzing the information read, instructors can help students to understand and to read more accurately themselves. This type of modeling of fluent reading promotes new information, important vocabulary, and opportunities for large and small group discussions (Trelease, 2001). An inclusive college instructor could, for example, take the role of a historical figure in reading aloud complex material. Then the students can be required to take opposition and debate the material, referring back to the text for support.

Another technique that improves fluency is to orally and visually preview the material to be read. This can be done using vocabulary, a visual organizer, pictures, or setting the stage through predicting or presenting the problem. Using these instructional techniques forewarns the reader about what is important, what to look for, or what might be the critical issue. It also generally motivates the reader to seek answers to the questions

TABLE 4.3. Template for the Question Exploration Guide—For Individual or Group Use to Guide the Reading Process

Main Question to be explored or Key Question:	
Key Vocabulary Terms:	
This section can be used to indicate sub-topics, secondary questions that underlie the main question, or minor concepts that support the main topic.	This section can be used to summarize the answers found in the reading, take notes, or indicate page numbers where the answers are located.
Template for K-W-L Chart- For Individual or Group Use To Guide the Reading Process	

What is already known about the topic	What you want to learn about the topic	What you actually learned about the topic

presented. An example of the preview strategy is the Question Exploration Guide. This instructional strategy (Salend, 2005, p. 348) is a variation of a KWL chart (What is already *known*, what is unknown and students *want* to learn, what is *learned* from the new material or readings). In the Question Exploration Guide, the critical question is identified, either by the college instructor or the students. Along with the critical question, key vocabulary is identified (see Table 4.3).

Students then read for the answers to the critical questions and develop questions of their own as they read along. The resulting information can be developed into a chart or outline of the material, thus allowing students to demonstrate their understanding of the concepts. Another possibility is to break large and complex reading assignments into more manageable parts with separate scoring guides and deadlines.

REMEMBERING AND RETRIEVING INFORMATION

Many of today's students have difficulty in remembering and retrieving information learned. In some cases, this is due to poor learning or understanding of the materials. Students often retain critical information long enough to take the test. The information is then quickly forgotten. In other cases, students may not have known good strategies for remembering content. In either case, college instructors need to use instructional strategies that increase retention and retrieval of information that were not used in the past. Using mnemonics can be a helpful instructional strategy for remembering information. *Mnemonics* is the use of an instructional strategy for remembering or aiding in the retrieval of information from LTM (Vaughn & Bos, 2009). It can be visual or auditory or both. Mnemonics should be used with information that is distilled or is in a framework format rather than large amounts of information.

There are several instructional ways to create mnemonics. One is to categorize the information to be remembered with previously-learned material. In this manner, the new material can be associated with a saying or phrase that will bring to mind the previously learned information. Another is to associate it with an acronym or saying, such as using the alphabet or a sequence of numbers. The third way is to use pegwords (Turnbull, Turnbull, & Wehmeyer, 2007, p. 271). A pegword mnemonic is to link the new material to rhyming words. Often rap music uses pegwords that rhyme with or stand for other words. One example is *jiggy* which means getting down with it or being OK with what is happening. So our founding fathers were jiggy with the idea that "All men were created equal." This pegword mnemonic stands for concept of equality in the Constitution and is remembered by the pegword of jiggy. Another variation is using the word *equality* as rhyming with *ideology,* thus bringing to mind the concepts of the founding fathers, the Constitution, or shared ideology, thus bringing to mind the concepts behind the term *equality.* By using the pegword, college students can understand and remember the associated new material.

Using pictures, cartoons, or visual depictions of materials is an excellent way to help students learn and retrieve information. Other chapters within this text (see Ch. 6 for further information) will discuss strategies for visualization of materials. However, the idea of using a single picture, with accompanying visual details, to convey a single concept is an excellent instructional strategy for remembering and retrieving information. Many students will process and remember information visually that they cannot process using text. Good visual mnemonics are simple, easy to recall, have pictures that are clear and easily identifiable, and utilize active learning to create (Turnbull, Turnbull, & Wehmeyer, 2007, p. 325). By teaching students to use mnemonics or to create their own personal mnemonics, instructors can help them to learn and retrieve critical information (Deschler, Ellis, & Lenz, 1996). The difficulty in the use of mnemonics is that sometimes the mnemonic itself comes to mind, but the learner is unable to recall what the code was used to remember. In this case, the most likely problem is that the mnemonic was not directly linked with corresponding text or pictures that represented the concept to be remembered.

Inclusive college instructors use of questioning can often help students to retrieve what was previously taught or to retrieve where in their learning process the concept is to be found (Fallon & Weinbeck, 2006). Questions can be used as prompts or cues and are effective in guiding group discussions. They also can promote deeper thinking and help the learners link the knowledge to previously learned material. Good questions need to be carefully formulated. There are a number of varieties of questions, such as:

- Questions that require simple recall of material;
- Questions that require understanding of material previously presented;
- Questions that require analysis of material;
- Questions that require evaluation of material;
- Questions that require synthesis of material; and
- Questions that require application of learned material.

Inclusive college instructors should consider whether the question should be open-ended or closed. They should decide in advance what questions are appropriate for group discussion and where in the course content that group discussion should take place. They should utilize sufficient wait time for answers. They should not pose multiple questions. Questions are more effective when they are used with time for thought and placed within the academic content to facilitate a deeper level of thinking. Using such questioning effectively particularly in group discussions, can be a rich source of information on the students' learning and what they understand about the subject matter.

Many students will spend significant amounts of their time in college classrooms listening to college instructors or classmates present academic information. However, many students learn more effectively using a visual approach than auditory means. Still, it is difficult for college instructors to limit that need to present content or to lecture. One technique to focus the listening process is for students to use note-taking strategies. Effective note-taking helps students to be actively engaged with the material, to better remember what was said, and to have information that can be studied for test taking purposes. Inclusive college instructors can assist their students in the note-taking process to make it more efficient and usable. Many college instructors use Power Point presentations to guide their lectures. Students can easily access a course management system for the Power Point and to convert them for note-taking purposes. Inclusive instructors should incorporate into their lecture some concepts that require students to interact with the Power Point slides. The students should be directed to summarize the concepts in their own words in the notes and to share them with other students in the class.

However, there are other steps inclusive college instructors can take. They can insert into class presentations some cues, such as "Get out your notes" or "This should go into your notes." Inclusive college instructors should allow sufficient time for students to write. They should record samples of students' notes into the course management system (see C h. 8 for additional information) to be shared with other students. Students should be encouraged to write phrases or to paraphrase, rather than trying to capture a complete, complex sentence. Inclusive instructors can suggest the consistent use of a format for note-taking. One example is the two-column format for taking notes (Strichart & Mangrum, 1993, p. 93). The left-hand side of the paper can be used for rough notes. The right-hand side can be used to note questions unanswered or to coordinate with text reading. Lines between notes should be skipped to show changes among concepts or ideas. Inclusive college instructors encourage the use of pictures or quick cartoons to depict actions or conflicts. These are visual instructional strategies that many students find effective.

Inclusive college instructors can add a summary review to the note taking strategy. The summary review takes place in the last five minutes of the class period. The critical concepts are named and briefly reviewed. The important vocabulary is highlighted. Inclusive instructors encourage their students to immediately adjust their notes to reflect the most important information and any information that was missed. The note-taking and the summary review instructional strategies can also be paired with the use of the advanced organizers discussed previously in this chapter. This combining of inclusive instructional strategies helps to ensure that all college students know and understand the most important academic concepts covered. Inclusive college instructors may also encourage students who have missed information to stay after class and get the misconception or missing information immediately corrected.

CONCLUSIONS

As inclusion continues to evolve in classrooms across the United States, instructors' beliefs and practices are still being challenged by the changes in the students who make up their college classroom communities. Learning to balance the teaching and learning process is the critical job of the college instructor. Many instructors use a director type of approach to teaching in the college classroom. However, to ensure that all students have access to the academic content, college instructors will have to change their approach to the teaching and learning process. They will need to make their role more of a facilitator of the learning process. This means to incorporate into their teaching instructional strategies that assist students to preview, organize, understand, remember, and retrieve critical concepts.

By incorporating these instructional strategies into their teaching, inclusive college instructors literally teach student how to learn and apply critical content to other content areas. Thus, students can apply the same techniques to their studying and the retrieval of the information in test situations. For inclusive college instructors, the ability to do self evaluation on their teaching practices is critical. A major influence upon inclusive instructors' sense of self as a professional is their ability to reflect upon their dispositions, knowledge, and professional skills using reflection and self analysis. Then, inclusive instructors can incorporate their self evaluations into making instructional changes that promote the learning of all students.

REFERENCES

Angelo, T.A., & Cross, K. P. (1993). *Classroom assessment techniques: A handbook for college teachers* (2nd ed.). San Francisco: Jossey-Bass, Inc.

Cox, M. (2004). Introduction to faculty learning communities. *New Directions in Teaching and Learning, 97,* 5–23.

Deschler, D. D., Ellis, E.S., & Lenz, B. K. (1996). *Teaching adolescents with learning disabilities: Strategies and methods* (2nd ed.). Denver, CO: Love Publishing Co.

Deschler, D. D., & Schumaker, J. B. (1986). Learning strategies: An instructional alternative for low achieving adolescents. *Exceptional Children, 52*(6), 583—590.

Dewey, J. (1900). *The school and society.* Chicago: University of Chicago Press.

Fallon., M., Halquist, D., & Balzano, B. (June, 2009). *Using evidence-based interventions to meet the needs of all learners: Teachers balancing curriculum and standards.* Paper presented at the first-ever international conference, The Practical: An East-West Curriculum Dialogue. Beijing, China.

Fallon, M., & Weinbeck, S. (March, 2006). *Teaching with Socratic questioning.* A presentation at the Center for Excellence in Learning and Teaching (CELT), College at Brockport., State University of New York, Brockport, NY.

Friend, M., & Cook, L. (2007). *Interactions: Collaboration skills for school professionals* (4th ed.). White Plains, NY: Longman Publishing Co.

Gardner, H. (1997). *Beyond multiple intelligences.* Keynote speech at the annual meeting of the Association for the Supervision and Curriculum Development. San Antonio, March 22.

Heward, W. L. (2009, 9th ed.). *Exceptional children: An introduction to special education.* Upper Saddle River, NJ: Pearson Education, Inc.

Lentz, B.K. (1983). Promoting active learning through effective instruction: Using advanced organizers. *Pointer, 27*(2), 11–13.

Salend, S. J. (2005). *Creating inclusive classrooms: Effective and reflective practices for all students.* Upper Saddle River, NJ: Pearson Education, Inc.

Schwab, J. J. (1983). The practical 4: Something for curriculum professors to do. *Curriculum Inquiry, 13*(3), 239–265.

Slavin, R. E. (2000). *Educational psychology: Theory and practice.* Boston: Allyn & Bacon.

Strichart, S. S., & Mangrum, C. T. (1993). *Teaching study strategies to students with learning disabilities.* Boston: Allyn & Bacon.

Trelease, J. (2001). *The read-aloud handbook* (5th ed.). New York: Penguin, Co.

Turnbull, A., Turnbull, R., & Wehmeyer, M.L. (2007). *Exceptional lives: Special education in today's schools* (2nd ed.). Upper Saddle River, NJ: Pearson Education, Inc.

Vaughn, S., & Bos, C. (2009). *Strategies for teaching students with learning and behavior problems* (7th ed.). Upper Saddle River, NJ: Pearson Education, Inc.

CHAPTER 5

THE CHANGING ROLE OF INSTRUCTORS AS BOTH LEADERS AND LEARNERS

Paul T. Parkison

KEY TERMS

Compliant Learners; Engaged Learners; Funds of Knowledge; Learning Path; Scaffolding

REFLECTIVE QUESTIONS

- How can college instructors facilitate a culture of engagement in which all students are encouraged to take intellectual risks?
- What skills do students require in order to engage with the college curriculum while recognizing the value of their personal experience and history?
- How can college instructors establish a classroom community in which learning is viewed by the students as a process that requires commitment and persistence rather than as an event that is experienced and credentialed?

Teaching Inclusively in Higher Education, pages 77–94
Copyright © 2010 by Information Age Publishing
All rights of reproduction in any form reserved.

OVERVIEW

Creating classrooms, courses, and instructional experiences that invite students to reflect upon and engage with the desired (or required) learning depends upon creating connections and relationships. Inclusive practice is essential to this process. Instructors in inclusive classrooms recognize the unique individual within each student and work to motivate students to participate by relating their individual experiences and perspectives with those reflected within the classroom community and curriculum. This requires instructors to recognize differences rather than ignoring them—to develop inclusiveness rather than striving for neutrality or segregation within the classroom and curriculum.

Instructors' perspectives toward the desired outcome, or role of the course, dramatically influence the impact courses can have for the students. Foucault's (1988) discussion of "caring for the self" presents a typology of technologies which provides instructors with an innovative method for preparing inclusive and engaging courses. Foucault's typology includes:

1. *Technologies of production,* which permit us to produce, transform, or manipulate things;
2. *Technologies of sign systems,* which permit us to use signs, meanings, symbols, or signification;
3. *Technologies of power,* which determine the conduct of individuals and submit them to certain ends or domination, an objectivizing of the subject; and
4. *Technologies of the self,* which permit individuals to effect by their own means or with the help of others a certain number of operations on their own bodies, souls, thoughts, conduct, and way of being, so as to transform themselves in order to attain a certain state of happiness, purity, wisdom, perfection, or immortality. (Foucault, 1988, p. 18)

How the instructors perceive the content and, importantly, the purpose of the course influence the technology for the care of self that the course is meant to develop. Introductory level courses can be easily classified as providing a set of tools that fall within the first and second levels of the typology: technologies of production and technologies of sign systems. The challenge arises as outcomes fall within the third and fourth categories: technologies of power and technologies of the self. Important questions regarding the changing role of instructors as both leaders and learners within higher education are raised by inclusive education when a "care of the self" perspective is considered.

Learning path refers to the process through which the level of thinking and the complexity of the content being learned emerge and are internalized by the learner. Focusing on the learning path helps to conceptualize the course and the learning that can occur as a result of the activities, materials, and expertise presented, as a process rather than as an end to be achieved. Learning path curriculum design encourages instructors to consider the experiences that are helpful in leading students from where their life experiences and received understanding have brought them toward the disciplinary understanding the course hopes to develop (Chappuis & Chappuis, 2008; Kansanen, 2003; Odora Hoppers, 2000; Stiggins, Arter, Chappius, & Chappuis, 2006; van Huizen, van Oers, & Wubbels, 2005). This approach to curriculum and course design requires that instructors recognize where each student is and then build from that position.

Funds of knowledge are the understandings and skills that have been accumulated throughout an individual's lifetime. These understandings vary across multiple factors that place an emphasis on the authentic experiences that individuals draw upon in order to make sense of the world around them. Gonzalez, Moll, and Amanti (2005) explain this understanding as "processual:"

> Processual approaches focus on the processes of everyday life, in the form of daily activities, as a frame of reference. These daily activities are a manifestation of particular historically accumulated funds of knowledge that households possess. Instead of individual representations of an essentialized group, household practices are viewed as dynamic, emergent, and interactional. (Gonzalez, Moll, & Amanti, 2005, p. 41)

Students' funds of knowledge (Banks, 2006; Costa, 2008; Gonzalez, Moll, & Amanti, 2005) support schemas that help individuals make sense out of their experiences and personal histories. Each schema provides a set of microstructures that create a logically coherent worldview that the individual can use to reach what Jean Piaget referred to as "equilibrium" (1972). These microstructures are the result of the technologies of the care of the self that have been developed by the individual, both in formal and informal educa-

Figure 5.1. Recognizing Student Schema

tional settings. These structures are responsive to new experiences and can be enhanced and expanded as students fully participate in their education.

ENGAGING STUDENTS IN THE LEARNING PROCESS

Helping students become acquainted with a role that for many is unfamiliar presents a significant challenge (See Table 5.1 for recommended texts). For many students, schooling has been a series of obstacles to be overcome in order to receive the required credential in order to proceed to the next obstacle. This commodity-focused schooling paradigm, which is prevalent within K–12 settings, is demonstrated in the focus upon grades and minimum competencies for a minimum expenditure of resources.

Recognizing Student Learning Intent

For many students, education has become a matter of accumulating the required credit hours, within the required curricular domains, to earn a college degree. This desire is vocationally appropriate, but challenges the traditional paradigm in which higher education is meant to develop the flexibility, reflective disposition, and critical thinking required to be individuals with practical reason (McKernan, 2008). Concepts such as sequence,

TABLE 5.1. Recommended Texts

1. Davis, B., Sumara, D., & Luce-Kapler, R. (2008). *Engaging minds: Changing teaching in complex times* (2nd ed.). New York, NY: Routledge.

   Davis, Sumara, and Luce-Kapler offer an intriguing and informative investigation of how complexity and coherence theories of epistemology impact learning and teaching. Inclusive education requires consideration of curricula designed with multiple access points for diverse learners.

2. Riggs, E. G., & Gholar, C. R. (2009). *Strategies that promote student engagement* (2nd ed.). Thousand Oaks, CA: Corwin Press.

   Riggs and Gholar present an impassioned appeal to connect classroom experiences to students' desire and motivation to learn. Conation, courage, and character are hallmarks of engaged learners. Helping to develop these dispositions requires intentional planning and effort.

3. McKernan, J. (2008). *Curriculum and imagination: Process theory, pedagogy and action research.* London and New York, NY: Routledge.

   McKernan demonstrates how inclusive curriculum design requires a return, or re-engagement with the democratic ideal of school-based, or classroom-based curriculum development. McKernan's appeal to a caring pedagogy provides a base from which to build inclusive classrooms.

program, or area of study lose meaning within a commodity paradigm such as one based on the accumulation of credits. Education, when viewed as a means to an end, loses its ability to grapple with issues of complexity and to help students achieve a sense of coherence within their received understanding of the world.

In this way, the educational process has become a matter of compliance and fulfillment of requirements (Beane, 2005; Boostrom, 2005; Costa, 2008; Davis, Sumara, & Luce-Kapler, 2008; Zmuda, 2008). This compliance view of education does not require much from the students beyond recalling and recognizing key facts and skills, being able to paraphrase and summarize material provided by instructors, and following directions well enough to provide instructors with what instructors want. This compliance view requires normalizing lenses, disciplinary rules and understandings that stand for the normal, taken-for-granted manner of perceiving the world. The process of generating the received methodologies and ways of understanding, what has been called discipline-normalization (Foucault, 1972), has provided instructors a means by which to differentiate, or judge, the character, ability, and future capability of students. These normalized structures fall within the realm of technologies of power in the typology presented by Foucault (1988). Students respond by conforming to these technologies of power in hopes of being evaluated as proficient and thus being awarded credit and being presented to future employers as worthy. Recognition of this process and the implications of not examining these normalized understandings is crucial to the development of inclusive classrooms.

Desired student learnings that fall within the technologies of production, sign systems, and power have become central components of the educational system. Accreditation agencies as well as university offices of institutional assessment look for these behavior-based outcome statements routinely. Recognizing these as types of normalizing structures allow instructors to anticipate and mediate the separating tendencies that are inherent in these technologies. Developing uniform units of study can assist students in recognizing what they already know and can do, anticipating the types of experiences they will have within a course or activity, and planning for their intentional involvement in the learning process.

Compliant Learners

Compliant learners result from having learned throughout their schooling experience to conform to the expectations of their instructors and teachers. These students have become proficient at jumping through hoops in an effort to acquire certification which enables them to progress through the schooling system. Compliant learners are those students who simply follow directions and finish the necessary paperwork on time (Banks, 2006; Beane, 2005; Burbules & Berk, 1999; Haggis, 2008; O'Toole, 2008; Zmuda, 2008). They work like what Zmuda (2008) describes as low-level bureaucrats. Each assignment, experience, and activity is seen as one more task to be completed in order to receive credit—credits which are accumulated over time until enough are gathered to receive a diploma. Zmuda provides an indication of the impact instructors can have on the adoption or avoidance of the compliant learner position:

> Educators must reevaluate the degree to which compliance has affected every aspect of the learning environment, including the use of established classroom assessments and grading systems to identify success. Many *A* students have earned high marks primarily because of their meticulousness in following directions, their knack for repeating procedures on cue, and their ability to expertly summarize other people's ideas. (Zmuda, 2008, p. 38)

Compliant learners are a result of both instructors' expectations—instructors' expectations are for their students to know, comprehend, and apply what has been taught—and discipline normalization. Focus on learning outcomes can lead to instructors directing students to an expected result or predetermined learning outcome (Boostrom, 2005; McKernan, 2008). From this pedagogical perspective compliance is the path of least resistance for some students.

Engaged Learners

Engaged learners are those students who pursue their interests and curiosity in an effort to clarify their personal understanding. These students are independent learners who simply need a prompt and occasional support in order to pursue the development of their personal understanding. Engaged learners, students who question, challenge, and participate in the curriculum, present a particular yet significant challenge to college instructors (Beane, 2005; Boostrom, 2005; Davis, Sumara, & Luce-Kapler, 2008; O'Toole, 2008; Riggs & Gholar, 2009; Zmuda, 2008). Instructors must help them develop the skills necessary to investigate complex issues and experiences, compare those issues and experiences within disciplined modes of inquiry, and develop their preferences and identity according to intentional criteria (Beane, 2005; Dewey, 1916; Gadamer, 2001; O'Toole, 2008). Analyzing, synthesizing, and evaluating students' educational experiences in this way requires that inclusive college instructors consider the manner in which students have been introduced to these methods of investigation, comparison and evaluation. Have they been given the opportunity to respond to instructors' prompts? Have they been placed into situations in which they can choose among a variety of methods of investigation, comparison, and evaluation?

Focusing on issues of complexity and coherence changes the aim of education (Davis, Sumara, & Luce-Kapler, 2008; McKernan, 2008). Dewey (1916) discussed freeing education from the "tyranny of ends." Complexity and coherence require student engagement in a process that is free of predetermined and prescriptive ends or outcomes. Engaged learning requires that students recognize and reflect upon their received knowledge, skill, and dispositions as a starting point from which to achieve growth and learning (Burbules & Berk, 1999; Freire, 1994; Haggis, 2008; Hofer, 2006; Varela, 1999; Zmuda, 2008). Gadamer (2001) describes the relationship between a course of study and an engaged learner:

> It is of course quite clear that certain uniform units of study must be followed, but the decisive point is this: that one ultimately develops in teenagers the capability to overcome their lack of knowledge through their own initiative. Self-education must above all consist in this, that where one perceives one's shortcomings, one strengthens one's own resources (*Kräfte*) and that one does not relinquish this responsibility to the school, or rely on school grades, or on school reports or on whatever is given a premium by parents. (p. 535)

The "self-education" of engagement resembles autonomous or authentic learning as students are trained to deal with events and experience.

Essentially, engaged learners are looking for the opportunity to buy into the college experience and curricula. Again, Zmuda (2008) helps to characterize the engaged learners:

> Instead of focusing on the grade or score, they can focus on their progress. Instead of focusing on getting the assignment over with, they can find satisfaction during the creation and production of work. Instead of trying to eliminate or cover up mistakes, they can evaluate the source of the error and search for a potential insight about their understanding—or their misunderstanding—of the content, the discipline, or themselves. (Zmuda, 2008, p. 40)

Negotiating the distinction between course content that provides a set of tools that sustains hegemonic power relations among and between students and course content that provides a set of tools that enables students to engage in reflective practice, leads to a reconsideration of the role of instructors in higher education.

Power and course content are traditionally, as taken-for-granted processes, under the control of instructors as manifest in terms of the choices of instructional strategies and concepts to be taught. In this hegemonic paradigm, disciplinary norms and methods of inquiry, as well as the decisions regarding what counts as legitimate knowledge and what does not, are held as craft secrets and serve as the source of instructors' power and control.

Moving away from the paradigm is critical. For instructors, this shift in paradigm toward a more inclusive and learner-focused perspective is a daunting proposal. Moving toward a learning path curriculum design perspective will place the emphasis on empowering all students through instruction in the use and purpose of the disciplinary norms and methods of inquiry. All students are thus empowered to use these technologies to pursue their individual interests and concerns, to adapt their fund of knowledge to accommodate new experiences and insights. This leads to meeting the needs and interests of all learners. A significant alternative to the current hegemonic instructional paradigm emerges as the long-term needs and interests of the students are considered.

PLANNING FOR ENGAGED LEARNERS

Moving beyond a paradigm that views higher education as a means to an end (higher pay, social mobility, etc.) toward a paradigm that encourages reflective construction of knowledge, skills, and dispositions in an effort to bring coherence to students' complex lives requires the design of courses with engaged learning in mind. Developing higher-education experiences that are learning-centered requires an alternative role for instructors. Rather than developing curriculum with compliance as an outcome based exclusively on technologies of power, as mentioned earlier in this chapter (Foucault, 1988), strategies will be introduced to help instructors facilitate engaged learning classrooms. The development of higher-education experiences that effectively integrate curriculum, instruction, and assessment require a reconsideration of the role of instructors and students in this process.

Recognizing Funds of Knowledge

Students come to the higher-education classroom as compliant learners who require a coherent curricular experience that not only provides the tools they need for a successful future, but provides access and guidance to the accumulated knowledge that can help them understand their individual experience. Students need technologies of production and sign systems (Foucault, 1988) in order to communicate as receivers of knowledge and as creators of knowledge. Introductory-level curricula need to intentionally facilitate the development of these technologies. Many instructors feel that the development of these technologies falls within the purview of elementary and secondary education. Unfortunately for many students, their K–12 schooling utilizes tools that sustain the power relations among and between students, and fails to accomplish the objective for all students of providing the tools necessary to become engaged learners.

High-stakes testing and accountability create a paradigm in which students are encouraged to be risk averse and compliant (Parkison, 2009). Students need to learn how to engage with the learning experiences made available at the university. Engagement requires that students become responsible risk takers who search for connections and reflect upon their received understanding in relationship to new educational experiences. The private-space perspective, one based in the recognition of each student as an individual, is essential to teaching inclusively in higher education as students come to recognize the validity and value of their fund of knowledge, or their received cultural understanding and personal history, as curricular content (Gonzalez, Moll, & Amanti, 2005). Simultaneously, inclusive instructors must learn to use the students' multiple received understandings as pedagogical content that has value within the course and discipline.

Private Space Perspective

Focusing on the private space perspective requires observation and testimony regarding the students' thoughts, feelings, and actions. Students are recognized as authentic individuals as they discuss and participate in dialogue regarding their personal experience with classmates and instructors. This is essential if students are going to move beyond their received understanding and begin to internalize the course curriculum. The content of the students' lived experience serves as a constraint on their perspective and perception of the course of study being presented. This constraint can either be an inhibiting factor or an enabling factor depending upon the perspective and approach of instructors.

Recognition, as described by Honneth (1996, 2001), is important in enabling the students to develop a positive self-narrative and is a requisite for the development of agency within the classroom. Through recognition, students attain a positive and practical relation to self and their received knowledge, skill, and dispositions that are culturally, educationally, and experientially acquired funds of knowledge (Gonzalez, Moll, & Amanti, 2005). This process can be transformative for the students and is necessary for them to take advantage of the opportunities and manage the risks they will encounter in the future (Freire, 1970; Giroux & Searls-Giroux, 2004). When instructors adopt a perspective of separatism—a perspective that looks toward classifying individuals into diverse and essential categories— they promote a connection between diversity and individual deficiency. This deficit perspective is counter-productive within an inclusive classroom. When instructors maintain hegemonic control over the course content and process, the needs of learners are not only disregarded, but their funds of knowledge are framed as illegitimate. Inclusive classrooms and courses incorporate the students' experiences and understanding into the course content and processes.

Learning Path Curriculum Design

In Table 5.2 a curriculum projection template is presented that will guide instructors through the development of an inclusive and responsive course curriculum. Intentionally linking the curriculum, instruction, and assessment begins the process of developing learning path curricula. Each element requires instructors to recognize the funds of knowledge of all students and the discipline-normalization (or technology of power) that influence the structure of a specific course.

Desired student learning prompts instructors to pose a potential outcome or destination for the learning experiences facilitated along the learning path. McKernan (2008) explains a similar perspective as a process-oriented curriculum design strategy:

> My definition is similar in adopting a process rather than specifying the results of teaching and learning. A curriculum is a proposal setting out an educational plan, offering students socially-valuable knowledge, attitudes, values, skills and abilities, which are made available to students through a variety of educational experiences, at all levels of the education system. As a proposal, the curriculum is a hypothesis inviting a research response. (McKernan, 2008, p. 12)

TABLE 5.2. Learning Path Design Template

	Desired Student Learning		
Indicator:	Source of Learning Experience or Data	Learning Extension or Research	Assessment Plan Indicators
1.			
2.			
3.			

Utilizing Foucault's (1988) typology of care for self technologies, the desired student learning can be framed as an anticipated outcome, but one in which the dynamic complexity of the classroom emerges. This complex classroom climate develops within the in-between space where empowered individuals meet and interact. Both instructors and students are empowered within the space necessary for emergent learning to occur (Davis, Sumara, & Luce-Kapler, 2008). This sounds complicated but the difference is one of perspective rather than form.

Generating statements of desired student learning (whether as an individual instructor acting autonomously or as a faculty committee developing standardized outcomes) represents the fundamental first step in developing learning path curriculum. Three taxonomies have been developed that assist in the development of these statements. The cognitive domain refers to the sophistication of the required thinking that a question or lesson requires of a student or learner. This domain is explained best in the taxonomy of cognitive behavior developed by Bloom (1956). Within the same research series, the affective domain is described as the area of student learning characterized by student internalization and habituation of skills, procedures, and processes (Krathwohl, Bloom, & Masia, 1964). As motivation and engagement of students has emerged as a factor in understanding learning, the conative domain has evolved as a structure that helps clarify student attunement (Riggs & Gholar, 2009). Table 5.2 provides a brief overview of each of these taxonomies (see Table 5.2). Each presents a tentative hierarchy that can be used to develop learning path or trajectory through which student learning can be assessed. The determination of the appropriate tier of proficiency to be attained by the students (and the individual student) requires recognition of the initial fund of knowledge the students bring to the course, the level and role of the course within a program of study, and the instructor's assessment of appropriate learning achievement.

Typical statements of desired learning follow a common grammar. Desired learning statements, like learning outcomes or objectives, correspond to the following structure:

> The student will ... (cognitive, affective, or conative proficiency) ... content to be experienced (fund of knowledge, disciplinary knowledge, or experience)
> > Ex.: Students will prioritize and express preferences for their ethical obligations to others and their responsibility to contribute to the common good.

By focusing on the process to be learned (whether cognitive, affective, or conative in nature), it is possible to develop learning paths that recognize student proficiencies, differences, and progress. Beginning with a coherent and explicit statement of desired learning sets the process in motion.

Recognizing and identifying the cognitive, affective, or conative proficiency that will transfer within and between disciplines are significant criteria when developing statements of desired student learning (Marzano & Kendall, 2007).

Course curricula are structured around the complexity of lived experience and the received processes and structures (disciplinary knowledge) that have helped to construct meaningful and coherent webs of association that shape understanding (Davis, Sumara, & Luce-Kapler, 2008). Planning has an epistemology that can restrain instructors by subjecting them to a range of structural and behavior conditions. These structural and behavioral conditions serve a useful function however—they restrain the breadth of the course and provide a focus to the course's content. Disciplinary norms and the received knowledge base of the various disciplines provide a useful constraint—an enabling constraint—as instructors plan the course offerings. Inclusive education also acknowledges and recognizes the students' experiences and received knowledge as legitimate content for course investigation and discussion.

As students enter the classroom they bring with them coherent views of how their world works. They have learned through experience how to make sense out of the world and their surroundings. Recognizing this schema and its value to each student is critical. Piaget (1972) asserted that this individual world view is a result of equilibration or the search for balance and stability. As individuals have new experiences, they either assimilate the new experience as a coherent part of their existing world view, or they accommodate their world view to maintain their balance in relation to this new experience. The difference is analogous to that between being served a "turkey burger" vs. confronting a 9/11 event (the terrorist attacks on the World Trade Center in New York City and the Pentagon in Washington, DC). Most people would be familiar with the construct of ground meat on a bun and would have very little difficulty assimilating the experience of that meat being turkey rather than the more familiar experience of ground beef. Confronting perspective-changing experiences like those of 9/11/2001 requires individuals to accommodate an experience that does not fit their schema. They must change their schema in order to make sense of this dramatic, and potentially traumatic, experience.

Lev Vygotsky (1978) built upon this foundation and introduced the idea of *scaffolding* student learning by providing the appropriate supports for students as they are confronted by new experiences within the classroom—and potentially outside the classroom as well. Scaffolding supports the students as they move from their pre-course understanding of the world through and with a discipline-based understanding of the world. Focusing on how students think about the content of their lived experiences and the content of the specific course or sequence of courses depends upon in-

TABLE 5.3. Cognitive, Affective, Conative Taxonomies

Level	Cognitive Domain (Bloom, 1956)	Affective Domain (Krathwohl, Bloom, & Masia, 1964)	Conative Domain (Riggs & Gholar, 2009)
Tier One: Essential Introductory Proficiency	*Knowledge*: the fund of knowledge—whether from the students' lived experience or as specific subject area content—that students can recall or recognize.	*Receiving*: the awareness of or sensitive to the existence of certain ideas, material, or phenomena.	*Personal Discovery*: the development and recognition of the value of learning and the appreciation of self as a learner.
Tier Two: (Technologies of production and sign systems) Communication and utilization of the introductory proficiency with direction	*Comprehension*: the students' ability to summarize or paraphrase a new set of experiences as knowledge or content. *Application*: the students' ability to follow directions as they implement a new skill set while expressing new or existing knowledge.	*Responding*: commitment in some small measure to the ideas, materials, or phenomena involved by actively responding to them by participating.	*Transition*: the willingness to engage in leaning, to be open to change, and to produce quality work.
Tier Three: (Technologies of power) Self-directed utilization of the technologies being developed.	*Analysis*: the ability to develop criteria or factors that help group distinct items or events. *Synthesis*: the ability to create new categories based upon multiple criteria developed through distinct analyses.	*Valuing*: willingness to be perceived by others as valuing certain ideas, materials, or phenomena by voluntarily utilizing the technology. *Organization*: relating the technology to those already held within the fund of knowledge and bring it into a harmonious and internally consistent philosophy	*Transformation*: the willingness to commit to becoming one's personal best, engage in positive learning experiences, recognize the intrinsic value of learning, and to act on and through new learning.
Tier Four: (Technologies of the self) effect by the students' own means a certain number of operations so as to transform themselves in order to attain a certain state of happiness, purity, wisdom, perfection, or immortality	*Evaluation*: the ability to use analysis and synthesis to prioritize and express preferences based upon evidence and logical arguments.	*Characterization by Value*: to act consistently and in accordance with the values which have been internalized.	*Transcendency*: the ability to express ideas and issues that matter most, transition through and utilize alternative funds of knowledge, assert an ethical position, and encourage others to engage in positive learning experiences.

structors learning from and about the students and leading them through the course processes and content (Beane, 2005; Burbules & Berk, 1999; Costa, 2008; Freire, 1994; O'Toole, 2008; Parkison, 2005). Providing collaborative and supportive dialogue within the classroom becomes the primary function of instructors. Having a sense of the destination or desired learning that students should be capable of at the end of a course is essential to effectively instructing them in an inclusive manner. The learning path emerges as the route from where the students are, what understandings the students' funds of knowledge will support, and what potential scaffolding instructors must provide to reach the desired learning for a course or program.

Learning path curriculum design traces a route from the students' funds of knowledge through to the initial statement of desired learning and differentiates the potential performances of that learning by identifying specific indicators of student proficiencies. These indicators simply differentiate the complexity and hierarchy of the proposed curriculum and identify progressive steps, or tiers, leading to the desired student learning. If the desired student learning falls within the fourth tier (See Table 5.3) of a taxonomy then the learning path design strategy would look to determine exemplars of Tier 3, Tier 2, and Tier 1 student learning.

- Tier 4: Students will prioritize and express preferences for their ethical obligations to others and their responsibility to contribute to the common good.
- Tier 3: Students will develop criteria or factors that help group distinct ethical obligations to others and their responsibility to contribute to the common good.
- Tier 2: Students will summarize or paraphrase received theories of criteria or factors that help group distinct ethical obligations to others and that define perspectives on the common good.
- Tier 1: Students will recall the existence of certain ideas, material, or examples of ethical obligations to others and perspectives on the common good.

Each tier provides an indicator of where students' learning and funds of knowledge stand. Moving from "default inferences" to "reasoned inferences" is demonstrated as students move from Tier 1 through Tier 4 indicators (Marzano & Kendall, 2007, p. 38). These indicators allow instructors to assess the proficiency of the students and to make instructional decisions regarding what experience or experiences are needed as scaffolding to help the students continue along the desired learning path within the technology for the care of self being addressed.

In a common rubric form this learning path would look like the one presented in Table 5.4. Rubrics of this type are formative assessment tools and

TABLE 5.4.   Ethical Obligation Rubric

Learning Tier/ Criteria	Preliminary Understanding	Applicable Understanding	Analytic Understanding	Evaluative Understanding
Understanding of Ethical Obligation to Others	Students will recall the existence of certain ideas, material, or examples of ethical obligations to others and perspectives on the common good.	Students will summarize or paraphrase received theories of criteria or factors that help group distinct ethical obligations to others and that define perspectives on the common good.	Students will develop criteria or factors that help group distinct ethical obligations to others and their responsibility to contribute to the common good.	Students will prioritize and express preferences for their ethical obligations to others and their responsibility to contribute to the common good.

should lead to informed instructional decision making and responsiveness to all students. As instructors develop courses utilizing a learning path design strategy, each learning outcome can be accompanied by a formative assessment rubric like the one in Table 5.4 to aid in course decision-making.

In order to complete the learning path design, instructors need to consider three critical factors: sources of expertise and student learning experiences, sources of authentic learning experiences, and sources of evidence of student learning. Again, the limitations of the epistemology of planning need to be considered as instructors identify these factors. It is important to plan so that information is gathered regarding the students' engagement in:

1. Translating information into knowledge: comprehending the value of experience and history;
2. Extending knowledge through discursive processes to impact understanding; and
3. Demonstrating learning through application to new tasks and contexts.

Remaining flexible is essential in an inclusive classroom—all students need to have space and encouragement to develop their individual expressions of learning. Learning is particularly risky for students who have been marginalized. All students need to have assurance that the learning environment is safe in order to take the necessary responsibility for learning to occur. Each of these factors of engagement facilitates inclusive instructors leading students through engaged learning experiences.

CONCLUSIONS

Learning path curriculum design provides significant benefits to inclusive classrooms. Curriculum becomes inclusive by creating intentional spaces through which students become engaged learners, developing the technologies for the care of self (Foucault, 1988) that values and validates their existing funds of knowledge and empowers them. The development of an awareness and understanding of the technologies of power will enable all students to develop the technologies of self that enable lifelong learning. Instruction becomes responsive to the specific needs of the students who make up the inclusive classroom community. It meets the students where they are and develops experiences that encourage engagement (questioning, challenging, and participating) with curriculum. Instruction that utilizes projects, inquiry, discussion, and service introduces students to new, unnoticed, and unfamiliar ways of being in the world. Instruction for engaged learning also helps students to re-notice, reflect upon, and practice ways of being that have become common sense and habit. Learning path curriculum design enables instructors to select and design strategies that promote real learning for all students. Additionally, assessment becomes more about decision-making—what is the next relevant and valuable experience the students need and deserve to have—and less about grading. Assessment within learning path curriculum design recognizes and acknowledges what students can and know rather than focusing on deficits and deficiencies.

The shift in focus facilitated by learning path curriculum design makes it possible to shift what is valued within inclusive classrooms. Mastery of content becomes less important than mastery of cognitive process and disciplinary ways of knowing that characterize care for self technologies. Student buy-in becomes more relevant from this perspective. Recognition of the funds of knowledge and private space perspective of the students becomes a bridge to facilitate student buy-in—the essential factor in all learning. Engaged students transfer what is learned to other life and learning contexts and continue to grow as intentional learners. Inclusive classrooms require instructors who are able to learn and lead within classrooms devoted to facilitating intentional learners.

REFERENCES

Banks, J. (2006). *Cultural diversity and education: Foundations, curriculum, and teaching* (5th ed.). Boston, MA: Pearson.

Beane, J. (2005). *A reason to teach: Creating classrooms of dignity and hope—The power of the democratic way.* Portsmouth, NH: Heinemann.

Bloom, B. S. (Ed.). (1956). *Taxonomy of educational objectives: Classification of educational goals. Handbook 1: Cognitive domain.* New York, NY: David McKay Company.

Boostrom, R. (2005). *Thinking: The foundation of critical and creative learning in the classroom.* New York, NY: Teachers College Press.

Burbules, N. C., & Berk, R. (1999). Critical thinking and critical pedagogy: Relations, differences, and limits. In T. S. Popkewitz & L. Fendler (Eds.), *Critical theories in education: Changing terrains of knowledge and politics* (pp. 45–65). New York: Routledge.

Chappuis, S., & Chappuis, J. (2008). The best value in formative assessment. *Educational Leadership, 65*(4), 14–19.

Costa, A. L. (2008). *The school as a home for the mind: Creating mindful curriculum, instruction, and dialogue* (2nd ed.). Thousand Oaks, CA: Corwin Press.

Davis, B., Sumara, D., & Luce-Kapler, R. (2008). *Engaging minds: Changing teaching in complex times* (2nd ed.). New York, NY: Routledge.

Dewey, J. (1916). *Democracy and education.* New York: Macmillan.

Foucault, M. (1988). Technologies of the self. In L. H. Martin, H. Gutman, & P. Hutton (Eds.), *Technologies of the self: A seminar with Michel Foucault.* Amherst, MA: University of Massachusetts Press.

Foucault, M. (1972). *The archaeology of knowledge.* New York: Pantheon Books.

Freire, P. (1994). *Pedagogy of hope:Reviving pedagogy of the oppressed.* New York: Continuum.

Freire, P. (1970). *Pedagogy of the oppressed.* New York, NY: Continuum Publishing Company.

Gadamer, H. G. (2001). Education is self-education. *Journal of Philosophy of Education, 35*(4), 529–538.

Giroux, H. A., & Searls-Giroux, S. (2004). *Take back higher education: Race, youth, and the crisis of democracy in the post-civil rights era.* New York: Palgrage MacMillan.

Gonzalez, N., Moll, L. C., & Amanti, C. (Eds.). (2005). *Funds of knowledge: Theorizing practices in households, communities, and classrooms.* Mahway, NJ: Lawrence Erlbaum Associates, Publishers.

Haggis, T. (2008). Knowledge must be contextual: Some possible implications of complexity and dynamic systems theories for educational research. *Educational Philosophy and Theory, 40*(1), 158–176.

Hofer, B. K. (2006). Beliefs about knowledge and knowing: Integrating domain specificity and domain generality: A response to Muis, Bendixen, and Haerle (2006). *Educational Psychology Review, 18*(1), 67–76.

Honneth, A. (1996). *The struggle for recognition: The moral grammar of social conflict.* Cambridge, MA: Polity Press.

Honneth, A. (2001). Recognition or redistibution? Changing perspective on the moral order of society. *Theory, Culture and Society, 18*(2–3), 43–55.

Kansanen, P. (2003). Studying—The realistic bridge between instruction and learning: An attempt to a conceptual whole of the teaching—studying—learning process. *Educational Studies, 29*(2/3), 221–232.

Krathwohl, D. R., Bloom, B. S., & Masia, B. B. (1964). *Taxonomy of educational objectives: Handbook II: Affective domain.* New York: David McKay Co.

Marzano, R. J., & Kendall, J. S. (2007). *The new taxonomy of educational objectives* (2nd ed.). Thousand Oaks, CA: Corwin Press.

McKernan, J. (2008). *Curriculum and imagination: Process theory, pedagogy and action research.* London and New York: Routledge.

Odora Hoppers, C. A. (2000). The centre-periphery in knowledge production in the twenty-first century. *Compare, 30*(3), 283–291.

O'Toole, L. (2008). Understanding individual patterns of learning: Implications for the well-being of students. *European Journal of Education , 43*(1), 71–86.

Parkison, P. (2005). The move to a pluralistic political vision of education. *The Journal of Educational Thought , 3*(2), 135–148.

Parkison, P. (2009). Political economy of NCLB: Standards, testing and test scores. *The Educational Forum , 73*(1), 44–57.

Piaget, J. (1972). *To understand is to invent.* New York, NY: The Viking Press, Inc.

Riggs, E. G., & Gholar, C. R. (2009). *Strategies that promote student engagement* (2nd ed.). Thousand Oaks, CA: Corwin Press.

Stiggins, R., Arter, J., Chappius, J., & Chappuis, S. (2006). *Classroom assessment for student learning: Doing it right—Using it well.* Portland, OR: Educational Testing Services Assessment Training Institute.

van Huizen, P., van Oers, B., & Wubbels, T. (2005). A Vygotskian perspective on teacher education. *Journal of Curriculum Studies, 37*(3), 267–290.

Varela, F. (1999). *Ethical know-how: Action, wisdom and cognition.* Standford, CA: Standford University Press.

Vygotsky, L. (1978). *Mind in society.* Cambridge, MA: MIT Press.

Zmuda, A. (2008). Springing into active learning: Giving students ownership of learning. *Educational Leadership , 66*(3), 38–42.

CHAPTER 6

USING LANGUAGE SUCCESSFULLY IN THE COLLEGE CLASSROOM

Ellyn L. Arwood and Joanna R. Kaakinen

KEY TERMS

Brain-Based Learning; Concepts; Higher-Order Thinking; Neuro-Semantic Language Learning System; Patterns; Visual Language Methods; Visual Thinker

REFLECTIVE QUESTIONS

- Why do bright students come to college able to replicate material, but struggle with higher- order thinking skills?
- What are the characteristics of the new type of visual thinker?
- How can college instructors adjust their language and teaching styles to meet the learning needs of this new visual thinker?
- How does knowledge about brain-based learning provide insight to teaching visual thinkers in college?

Teaching Inclusively in Higher Education, pages 95–112
Copyright © 2010 by Information Age Publishing

INTRODUCTION

Approximately 85% of today's adult students think in the cognition of "seeing what others say" rather than "hearing what others say" (Arwood & Kaakinen, 2009; Arwood, Kaakinen, & Wynne, 2002). This "visual thinking" (Arwood, Kaakinen, & Wynne, 2002) does not represent a visual learning style or preference but the actual way students' neuro-biological systems create meaning for their thinking or meta-cognition. Note that learning styles refer to educated preferences and this article is referring to learning as a neurobiological set of brain-based processes or *brain-based learning*. Synthesizing the literature on the relationships among brain-based learning, language, and cognition (e.g., American Psychological Association, 2002; Begley, 2007; Calvin, 1996; Carruthers, 1997; Gazzaniga, 2005; Goldberg, 2001; Goldblum, 2001; Greenfield, 1997; Greenough, Black, & Wallace, 1987; Naugle, Cullum, & Bigler, 1998; Siegel, 2007; Singh & O'Boyle, 2004; Wallace, Ramachandran, & Stein, 2004; Webster, 1999) provides an understanding of how college students construct meaning from their courses. Meaning literally occurs from the way that input is processed through the central nervous system which is the *neuro-semantic language learning system* (Arwood & Kaakinen, 2009). In other words, most of today's students (Arwood, 1992, 2005; Wilcox, 2007) think with a "visual brain system" that is different from the assumed "auditory brain system" (Arwood & Kaulitz, 2007) which parallels the sound-based approach to most teaching, such as lecture.

Most instructors teach in the properties of an auditory, sound-based language, therefore a mismatch exists between how most students think and how most instructors assume that students construct conceptual meaning. The purpose of this chapter is to help instructors: 1) understand the brain-based learning characteristics of a *visual thinker* so as to understand why classroom strategies must match students' ways of thinking (Arwood & Kaakinen, 2009); and 2) develop inclusive language-based teaching strategies so as to redesign auditory teaching and curriculum practices to match students' visual ways of thinking.

WHO ARE THESE VISUAL THINKERS?

College instructors often lament the loss of students who do not emulate the instructor, "Students are not like we were when we were in college…" or "When I was a student…" These types of comments stem from the fact that instructors typically use a sound-based or auditory way of teaching which does not match the way most students think. This mismatch between student learning and faculty teaching may mask the instructor's interpretations of students' behaviors. For example, the typical college student comes ready "to see what is said" instead of "hear what is said." Therefore, when students talk among themselves and busy themselves with other tasks during class instead of listening to the discussion, lecture, or presentation; the instructor thinks that the students are not attending. Likewise, the instructor may query why bother to painstakingly answer a student's question only to be asked the identical question from another student just moments later. Even in classes where there is little lecture, some students politely, but assertively complain about the drone of the "talking head spewing wah, wah, wah."

College instructors often believe that students are not able to use their own words to express ideas. For example, students ask for the instructor's notes or Power Point presentation handouts so they can replicate them on a test or assignment. Students want to know the exact content of test questions and answers. Students express more comfort and receive high academic marks when the purpose of the assignment is to only spew back memorization of patterns, such as the words in the text class notes, and/ or the exact words from the lecture. These same students plagiarize at an alarmingly high rate; and, when asked why they copied, they almost always say, "I didn't know I was copying because I changed a word or two." At the end of the semester, these same bright students admit on the course evaluation forms that they did not read or buy the texts. These students sometimes complain that the instructor talked too much and/or too fast, the reading was confusing, or other students asked too many questions. The aforementioned behaviors are created because of the mismatch between the instructor's auditory teaching and the students' visual thinking systems. Students can learn to think in their own words and *concepts*; however, they need instructors who understand how the students learn and process new information.

Perplexed by the irony of brilliant students who don't seem to understand the spoken language, but who can obtain perfect scores on standardized tests, instructors might ask, "How are these students learning?" "Why do these very bright students not listen to sound or read the text?" "If these students do not use the sounds of language for reading, writing, listening, viewing, thinking, then what do they use for learning?"

CHARACTERISTICS OF THE VISUAL THINKER

Understanding the characteristics of a visual thinker provides instructors with the basis for adjusting teaching methods. Visual thinking involves different neurobiological processes than thinking in sound. Most visual thinkers are not able to make higher-order meaning out of the instructor's spoken words, make meaning from the words in their texts, and write their ideas from the mental sound of words.

Students who think in a visual form of cognition possess the following specific characteristics (Arwood & Brown, 2001):

1. They create mental concepts using visual graphics like pictures, movies, or print instead of thinking in the sound of their own voices;

2. They can imitate exactly what they hear such as playing back the instructor's voice (phonographic memory) without necessarily understanding the words;

3. They are able to make an exact mental picture, like a photograph, that they can mentally recall; and

4. They organize and plan based on a spatial perspective of events rather than by an internal sense of time.

Each of these characteristics has an effect on how the student performs in the college classroom.

Since visual thinkers use mental pictures or graphics for conceptual learning, they must be able to mentally see how ideas connect contextually. Their pictures will not make a mental graphic until they possess all of the individual concepts which are contextually ordered. For example, a psychology instructor starts class by saying, "Individuals who suffer from OCD (obsessive compulsive disorder) are often stigmatized by society." To be able to understand what the instructor is talking about and what the whole class will cover, a visual thinker must have mental pictures about OCD to be able to understand the instructor's words. When a concept, such as OCD, is "helicoptered" into the students' brains in this auditory way, the instructor's words are out of context or in isolation unless the students already have significant understanding from personal experiences, such as having a family member with OCD. Sometimes, personal knowledge may even be negative, such as having heard derogatory jokes about people with OCD on the radio.

Without prior context, visual thinkers must translate the instructor's sound-words into accurate mental pictures in order to understand the spoken words. If the content of the course is new and the visual thinker cannot translate the sound of the instructor's words into mental pictures, then the whole lecture has little meaning.

Students who think with visual meta-cognition are able to separate the sounds of the instructor's voice from what they mentally or physically see. Therefore, when an instructor talks, students are able to mentally record exactly what the instructor says. Later, students are able to retrieve that recording and mentally hear the words just like the instructor spoke. For example, visual thinking students are often able to look at a test question and remember the exact sound of the instructor's voice talking about the topic.

In this way, the students are able to select the spoken words and match the words to the test questions to produce the correct answers. This is a form of acoustic imitation matched to visual pattern recognition. The students do not necessarily understand the conceptual meaning of the material.

Similarly, students who think with visual meta-cognition are able to look at a page and create a mental photograph of what they see. In this way, they are able to recall those pages for a test, just as if they had their physical notebook or text book open. This is a form of imitation; and, again, does not indicate that the students conceptually understand the material.

Visual thinkers see themselves in relationship to where they are and what they are doing. Some students mentally see themselves in relationship to the day, the week, or the whole term. If they see themselves by the day, then they will look at their assignments that are "due" the night before. If they see themselves by the week, then they will plan for assignments a week in advance. Or, if they think of themselves by the term, then they will plan their assignments by the semester. Thus, students begin to "do" an assignment when it is "due." These references to days, weeks, and terms are not time-based, but are space-based. In other words, students work according to what they see in their paper organizers, not according to an internal understanding of how much time the instructor has given for an assignment to be completed. The instructor may assign a term paper that a student with an assignment book set by the day begins the night before. This student might even complain that there was not have enough time for the assignment and ask for an extension.

TEACHING APPLICATIONS

Teaching practices can be designed to match both visual and auditory thinkers. Note that the term "visual and auditory thinkers" refers to how people neuro-semantically acquire concepts through brain-based learning, not the preferred or taught learning styles. Therefore, instructors who change their teaching practices to meet the visual thinkers will reach both auditory and visual thinking students. The auditory thinking students will learn from the instructor's talking because those students possess an auditory meta-cognition. The visual thinking students will more likely be included into the classroom because the instructors are providing visual strategies that match these students' meta-cognition. If instructors choose to not add visual strategies to their teaching then those who think with visual meta-cognition are more likely to be marginalized. To be inclusive, instructors must add visual language-based methods that meet the needs of the 85% of students who conceptually learn visually (Arwood, Kaakinen, & Wynne, 2002). The authors refer to these adjustments in the teaching as *visual language methods* or viconic language methods (VLMs) (Arwood, Kaulitz, & Brown, 2009).

The term VLM was developed to describe those practices that superimpose knowledge about visual cultural characteristics onto English; given that English is an auditory, time, and sound-based language (Arwood et al., 2009). In this way, the dominant culture is auditory in practice, but the majority of students think with a visual mind. A visual mind utilizes the context of ideas instead of spoken words for creating concepts. So, the VLM are based on the development of concepts for learning instead of the definition, categorization, and memorization of words. All of the applications presented in this section are based on VLM. As visual thinkers are able to access the content more easily, they are able to provide more than just memorized *patterns* or plagiarized works; they are able to think in a higher, more abstract thinking. In other words, they can synthesize content and put others' ideas into their own language for more depth in thinking.

RECOMMENDATIONS FOR CLASSROOM TEACHING

These recommendations are based on understanding how characteristics of visual languages provide insight to visual thinking. Each characteristic of a visual language like Mandarin can be used as a way to add visual properties to a classroom lesson. Each recommendation provides a way for an instructor to create more visual meaning for those students who think with visual properties (which is about 85% of all students).

Put Students in Their Pictures

Since the learning of new concepts always begins with what students already know, then it is important to teach new concepts with the students in their mental pictures (Arwood & Kaakinen, 2009). This level of cognitive development is pre-operational in nature as this level of thinking refers to the students' pre-existing mental information. Instructors can take difficult concepts that students do not have much pre-requisite knowledge and decrease the difficulty of the content just by placing the students into their own pictures of how they relate to the taught concepts. For example, instructors draw a picture of who the students are at the very beginning of the day's class. A nursing faculty might draw a small stick figure of a nurse in the corner of a dry-erase board (see Figure 6.1). The stick figure has a thought bubble and the instructor might say, "Questions that nurses typically think about when assessing heart rate include...." This puts the nursing students into their own mental pictures of themselves as nurses in relationship to the

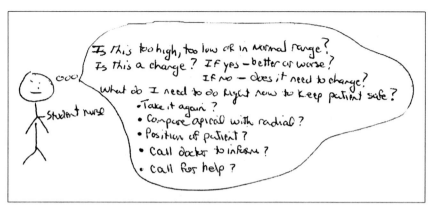

FIGURE 6.1.

concepts that are being taught. All disciplines have people who the students can relate to such as scientists, historians, authors, mathematicians, educators, musicians, engineers, business owners, and so forth.

Draw Concepts in Real Time.

Drawing in real time is a process of showing the concepts. It is not art. For students to develop their own mental visual graphics about the meaning of the concepts being taught, the students must be able to see how the concepts relate to one another. So, the instructor draws the concepts while simultaneously talking about the concepts. This strategy is called drawing in real time. Drawing in real time also provides students with the opportunity to see how connections among concepts are developed. An important aspect of this strategy is that some visual thinkers need to see the instructor's hand move to create those concepts. Figure 6.2 shows an example of a finished dry erase board that Kaakinen drew in real time. Inclusive instructors should note that just looking at the finished product does not provide much meaning, but students who watched the drawing were still, quiet, engaged, and able to perform better in discussion, tests, and follow-up assignments because they were able to learn through the way that they conceptualize.

Draw Visual Flowcharts

Notice that in Figure 6.3 the concepts relate to various ideas. Each time a connection between two or more ideas is made, an arrow is drawn to show

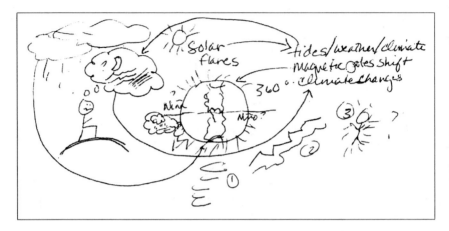

FIGURE 6.2.

the *higher-order thinking* that results from considering two or more concepts in relationship to one another. The result may be several connected flow charts. In Figure 6.3, the flowchart relates the concepts of the bell shaped curve to various testing parameters. This is only one drawing in a series of drawings about applications related to the bell shaped curve.

Note that this visual flow chart creates context through pictures that are connected, not just words in boxes connected by lines. The pictures are

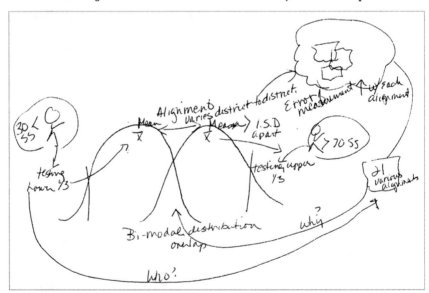

FIGURE 6.3.

about what the students think, whereas the written words are often patterns or imitated copy without conceptual understanding. College students are very adept at regurgitating or producing patterns but do not necessarily understand the concepts. Remember that drawing represents thinking and students must use their thinking to represent their ideas, so the students must draw their thoughts into their notes. In this way, the students are using their own language about the content so as to learn the material. If the instructors pass out their flowcharts or if students copy down the instructors' flow charts without thinking about the meaning and then putting the drawings into the students' thoughts, then the students will only be able to imitate or copy the instructors' ideas. Ideas are stored in semantic or long-term memory when language is added to the thinking.

Draw Cartoons

Some topics lend themselves to procedural or sequential types of knowledge. Cartooning this type of knowledge provides the students opportunities to see themselves in a psychomotor task such as an experiment, a lab activity, a practicum, an engineering design, a public presentation, a debate, and so forth. Figure 6.4 provides an example of a science experiment set of procedures.

Introduce Lessons with "I" Stories

The purpose of an "I story" is to provide a context for the students to see how they fit in the classroom content. For example, "Yesterday evening I was sitting on my back porch watching the sun set. I began to wonder why the horizon sky was so orange when it was more yellow the night before. So,

FIGURE 6.4.

I wondered if the air quality in my town affected what we see as 'color' in the sky. What sort of air quality factors do you think I should explore?" This "I" story can now go into a lesson on ecology, climate control, environmental policy, regulatory policy, business ethics, air pollutants, asthma, living in cities, and so forth. Here is another example, "This morning I was reading the newspaper which had an article about the high school graduation rate for 2008 being closer to 68% rather than the previously reported 84%. I was shocked! I wondered how could such a discrepancy happen? What do you think are some of the reasons for this mismatch between the actual graduation rate and the previously reported rate?"

Engage in Story-telling

For many years, good instructors were often those who told a lot of stories (Selsor, 2004; Simmons 2002). Stories provide visual thinkers with mental movies that attach to the concepts of the day. Therefore, for the story to work, the story has to have a clear purpose and a clear beginning-middle-end. The story must highlight the specific concepts of the day's lesson. And, at the end of the story, the instructor must retag or restate the critical concepts the instructor wants the students to learn. Stories should never exceed 10 minutes because this is the maximum length of time that students will be able to stay with the oral, spoken language and still connect to the mental visual concepts being taught.

INSTRUCTOR PREPARATION

In order to teach from a conceptual viewpoint, instructors must possess a deep level of knowledge about their content. Instructors must be able to sort out what concepts are "enduring" and "critical to know" from the fun, interesting, and nice to know facts about the concepts (Wiggins & McTighe, 2005). Therefore, before creating specific course presentations or classes, the instructor must spend time thinking about how the concepts connect and build from the developmental point of learning a new concept to understanding the new concept in application. In this way, the instructor must determine the best way for students who know nothing about the topic to learn the content. Instructors do not need to sample students' language to determine how their students think. Because the majority of students are visual thinkers and because instructors still talk even though they are drawing, then instructors may assume that most students will benefit from the inclusive practice of using Viconic Language Methods within the college classroom.

Rather than be guided by the order of content as outlined in a text book or by the order of class topics of a previous syllabus, instructors must determine what the visual thinker needs to be able to make mental pictures or movies of the new concepts. For example, most text books are designed by category: a nursing book might have a chapter on fluid management. Within that chapter, multiple concepts about different cardiovascular problems are broken down into sections covering assessment, outcomes, interventions, evaluations, and applications. This means that the students must be able to mentally carry the written words about a specific fluid problem like excess fluid volume through and across the various sections in order to build a conceptualization of how one assesses fluid volume, what is the norm, what to do for intervention, how to evaluate the interventions, and how to pull together and mentally summarize the data across these sections for a specific patient. So, the concepts are spread across the categories instead of being organized into a set that collectively relates the concepts into a big picture. Visual thinkers would understand the fluid management problem better if everything about excess fluid volume, for example, were connected to create a unified picture.

It is the instructor's responsibility to understand the material well enough that the instructor can present the course in a way for students to be able to make mental visuals that build their concepts. Instructors are accountable for adapting their teaching styles to meet the students' learning needs. Even though both authors are auditory thinkers, they have learned that teaching college students is about meeting the students' needs, not teaching in a way that is comfortable to the instructor.

Once the instructor has organized the content into sets that relate the material together so that students are able to build mental pictures about the content, then the instructor needs to prepare her own notes. Figure 6.5 shows an example of Kaakinen's thinking when preparing to draw in real time for her students. Note that the author wrote out her notes to compare the two types of fluid volume problems in an auditory way. Then the author drew the concepts as visual notes. Figure 6.6 shows these visual notes. The author takes these visual notes along with her auditory notes to class so that she can use both to draw in real time the concepts for the students (Arwood, E., Kaakinen, J., & Wynne, 2002).

In addition to preparing the content, the instructor also must help the students focus on what will be meaningful. The following includes some of the possible strategies that instructors prepare:

- Limit the focus before class reading to those concepts further explicated in class so that students come to class with some mental pictures.
- Provide the students with suggestions about how to look at pictures, graphs, and other visuals in the written material in order to develop visual meta-cognition.

Comparing Signs & Symptoms of Fluid Volume Excess + Deficit: Auditory Notes.

	Fluid Volume Excess	Fluid Volume Deficit
Brain	Δ mental status ↑ anxiety	Δ mental status: headache, ↑ICP, irritable, restless
eyes	blurred vision, periorbital edema	sunken, dry, ↓ tears
jugular vein	distended	normal
lungs	dyspnea ↑RR crackles, ↑fluid	no change – normal
BP	↑ hypertension	↓, orthostatic hypotension
pulse	bounding	weak
cap refill	≥3sec	<3sec normal
abdomen	sacral edema 3rd space	normal
urine	dilute, diuresis SG <1.010	↓ volume, SG >1.030, concentrated, amber
edema	pitting extremities	normal
weight	gain	loss

FIGURE 6.5.

- Suggest appropriate videos or links such as those on YouTube that will highlight specific concepts so that students are help to develop more examples of concepts so as to increase their depth of visual knowledge.
- Design authentic applications such as case studies that allow students to see themselves in the story.

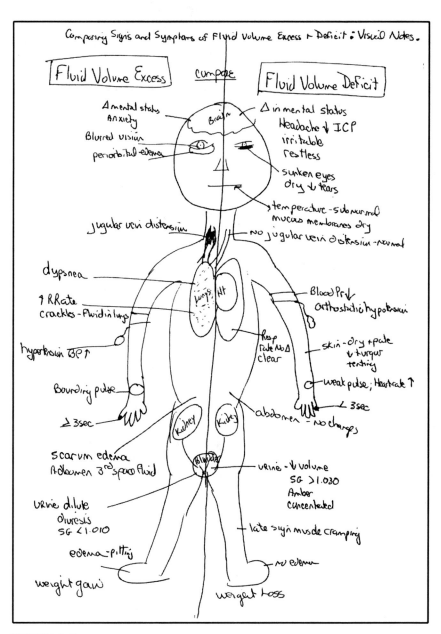

FIGURE 6.6.

STUDENT PREPARATION

Students expect to learn the way they have been previously taught. Since the type of teaching that is recommended in this chapter is different from what many students have experienced, these authors believe that the students also need to know how to study smarter, not harder. In other words, instructors explicitly tell students how to prepare for class in ways that also match the way students think. The following is a list of suggestions that instructors may use for helping students prepare for class:

- Share with the students how the class relates to the big picture of study related to the discipline so that students can make mental connections to what they are learning.
- Explain how the instructor's planned assignments connect to build the students' concepts from simple to complex.
- Discuss with students why investing time in developing their metacognition will help them learn concepts that they will be able to store and retrieve at a later time.
- Explain to students how to use their out-of-class assignments such as readings for creating visual concepts that they can draw, write, talk about.

SUCCESS DURING CLASS

The following is a list of suggestions that instructors may use during the class to help students be successful:

- Encourage students to sit where the material on the board or the instructor's mouth is to the side they write with. For example, if the student is right handed and the material is difficult to understand, then the student may want to sit on the left side of the room so that the material at the front of the room is to the student's right side. This strategy helps minimize the number of times that the brain must process the information.
- Encourage students to use the strategies that match with their learning system. For example, some students will want to watch the instructor and draw and write their own notes in their notebooks while other students may be encouraged to draw what the instructor draws. Students who think with the sound of their own voice will want to listen to the instructor's words. For some students, the instructor's talking or the other students' talking will interrupt the visual thinking. These students may need to learn how to turn-off the sound mentally while focusing on the visuals by drawing what they see. Also, during tests or quiet activities, instructors need to learn to not talk to students while students are trying to create their thoughts.

- Some students may prefer to wiggle or fidget or snack to help keep their pictures cognitively moving. These students can be encouraged to use these coping skills as long as they do not bother other students. If the fidgeting and snacking is getting in the students' own way of making pictures or making other students' thinking or pictures go away, then the students can be encouraged to use a pencil to doodle, draw concepts, and/or write to engage in a motor task that is less intrusive.

- Instructors suggest that students take the classroom material and put it into their own language. Students are able to think about the instructor's content during class; but, unless the students put their own language to the instructor's thoughts, the material will not go into long term memory. Without putting their own language to the content, students may be able to replicate the instructor's ideas, but not necessarily understand the concepts or recall the concepts for later use. For some content, students may be able to do this during class; for new content, students may need to do this out of class.

REDESIGN AUDITORY OR SOUND-BASED CURRICULUM PRACTICES

To turn a classroom lesson from an auditory type of lesson to a visual type of lesson, the instructor must think about the characteristics of a visual thinker. English is an auditory language which uses the alphabetic properties of words as the basis of the language. Therefore, auditory or sound-based curricula value the use of words. For example, outlines or organizational graphics use words without context and are therefore auditory in nature. The words are not connected to ideas that allow the visual thinker to connect their visual mental cognition to the isolated word. An example of the use of words without context is the use of Power Point presentations. The words on the Power Point belong to the instructor and are not connected to the mental visual thoughts of the student. Furthermore, many visual thinkers cannot utilize the instructor's spoken words that go with the Power Point. Any discussion that occurs in the dark while the Power Point is shown may also be lost since the visual thinker cannot see the speakers' mouths. Projecting visual images as examples of ideas that cannot be told with words such as brain MRI images, maps of battles, cell structures, mathematical derivatives, have purpose for a visual thinker in that they provide a picture of content. However, the content for these visual images must still be provided in a visual way if the student is to "see" and "understand" what they are looking at (Arwood & Kaakinen, 2004). For example, a photograph of a cellular structure is meaningful to the students who understand what they are looking at. To a student who does not have the concepts for what is in the photograph, the picture is just another beautiful slide. Spoken or writ-

TABLE 6.1. Auditory language lessons compared to visual language lessons

Auditory Language Approach to Curriculum	Visual Language Approach to Curriculum
Lecture format	Draw concepts in real time (see Figure 6.2)
Periodic overhead with oral explanations	Details connected to drawn concepts
Outline notes of the lecture	Students take their own visual notes
Flow chart of words (e.g., sickled RBC—vaso-occlusion—local hypoxia—tissue ischemia-infarction)	Drawings in real time explain the relationship between words and concepts (talk while drawing)
Use a visual graphic, which is an auditory metaphor (e.g., "imagine bee bees in a tube vs. jacks in a tube" for teaching the normal round red blood cells [RBC] vs. sickle RBC)	Draw the connections between the concepts that demonstrate the difference between normal round RBC and when RBC sickle under stress or changes in the body
Assign reading (e.g.,chapter) before class	Preview chapter before the class and read specific sections after the class

ten sound-based words about these images may not be processed by visual thinkers. The photograph is more meaningful to the visual thinker if the instructor draws the concepts of the cellular structures in real time so that when the students see the photograph they "know" what they are seeing. Table 6.1 provides the reader with a comparison between college content taught as auditory lessons or taught as visual lessons.

EDUCATION FOR HIGHER-ORDER THINKING

The rationale for meeting the visual thinker's learning needs is twofold: 1) higher education should prepare students to think and not just perform well for grades; and 2) higher education must meet the way a student thinks in order for students to develop conceptual meaning (Young, 2007), not just regurgitate patterns. For higher-order thinking of new concepts, visual thinkers need to create their own visual concepts that they can talk or write about in their own language.

Likewise, auditory thinkers must be able to use their sound words to create the language of their thinking. Instructors must allow for all students to represent their thinking in conventional ways. For example, all mental visuals are unique to the learner so allowing students to turn in a collage for higher-order concepts such as "community of learners" does not represent a formal way of thinking. The only shared or conventional form of thinking for all learners of English is the written form. Therefore, writing essays about conceptual understanding of content should be an important outcome of college lessons.

CONCLUSIONS

The new visual-thinking students come to college with an auditory style of coping, such as writing down the exact spoken words of the instructor or asking for the Power Point notes. These incoming college students have not learned how to use their own visual learning systems for higher-order thinking. Likewise, college instructors use methods based on auditory language properties, even when they are visual thinkers, because they teach the way that the dominant culture interprets the concepts of English, an auditory language. Unfortunately, the majority of instructors use an auditory teaching style, but the majority of students think with visual learning systems. This mismatch between teaching and thinking frustrates the instructors and marginalizes the students. If instructors want to provide inclusive practices for their students, then they must change their teaching practices to include more of their students in conceptual learning.

Inclusive college instructors recognize that 85% of their students are visual thinkers. Therefore, they draw in real time the concepts they are teaching so that students can see the visual concepts come to life. Meanwhile the inclusive instructor also teaches the visual thinkers to draw their own ideas into graphics, icons, picture flowcharts, etc., to represent the visual language of the content. Meanwhile the auditory thinkers listen to the stories told by the inclusive instructor who draws the content while telling the story of the content. The auditory thinkers put the college instructor's words into their own sound language. In both ways, the students are able to learn formal concepts. For both types of students, testing is at the formal level and students are able to recall and retrieve what they learn because they are using language to record the concepts in semantic memory. It is incumbent on inclusive instructors to base their teaching on how students learn. Likewise, it is important that instructors use guided evidence-based action research to determine ways to incorporate the new visual thinkers into the classroom through inclusive practices.

REFERENCES

American Psychological Association (2002). *Psychologists draw an 'architecture of attention,' outlining three brain-based building blocks,* October 14.

Arwood, E. (1992, 2005). Unpublished videotapes of college learning-language student interviews.

Arwood, E., & Brown, M. (2001) *A guide to visual strategies for young adults.* Portland, OR: APRICOT, Inc.

Arwood, E., & Kaakinen, J. (2004).Visual language strategies for innovative teaching of science. *Journal of Science Education for Students with Disabilities, 10,* 27–31.

Arwood, E.L. & Kaakinen, J.R. (2009) SIMulation Based on Language and Learning (SIMBaLL): The model. *International Journal for Nursing Education Scholarship, 6*(1), art. 9.

Arwood, E., Kaakinen, J., & Wynne, A. (2002) *Nurse educators: Using visual language.* Portland, OR: APRICOT, Inc.

Arwood, E., & Kaulitz, C. (2007) *Learning with a visual brain in an auditory world: Language intervention strategies for individuals with autism spectrum disorders.* Shawnee Mission, KS: Autism Asperger Publishing Company.

Arwood, E., Kaulitz, C., & Brown, M. (2009). *Visual thinking strategies for individuals with autism spectrum disorders: The language of pictures.* Shawnee Mission, KS: Autism Asperger Publishing Company.

Arwood, E., & Young, E. (2000). *Language of RESPECT.* POD Amazon or Barnes & Noble. Portland, OR: APRICOT, Inc.

Begley, S. (2007). *Train your mind: Change your brain.* New York: Ballantine Books

Calvin, W. H. (1996). *How brains think: Evolving intelligence then and now.* New York: Basic Books.

Carruthers, S. A. (1997). *Language, thought, and consciousness: An essay in philosophical psychology.* Cambridge, UK: Cambridge University Press.

Gazzaniga, M. S. (2005) *The ethical brain.* Washington, D.C.: Dana Press.

Goldberg, E. (2001). *The executive brain: Frontal lobes and the civilized mind.* New York: Oxford University Press.

Goldblum, N. (2001). *The brain-shaped mind: What the brain can tell us about the mind.* Cambridge, UK: Cambridge University Press.

Greenfield, S. A. (1997). *The human brain: A guided tour.* New York: Basic Books.

Grenough, W. T., Black, J. E., & Wallace, C. S. (1987) Experience and brain development. *Child Development, 58,* 539–559.

Naugle, R: Cullum, C. M., & Bigler, E. D. (1998). *Introduction to neuropsychology: A case book.* Austin, TX: PRO-ED, Inc.

Selsor, K. (2004). Stories persuade and motivate. *Brain Store Newsletter. 6(2),* Feb. 2.

Siegel, D. J. (2007). *The mindful brain.* New York: Norton.

Singh, H. & O'Boyle, M. (2004) Interhemispheric Interaction during global-local processing in mathematically gifted adolescents, Average ability youth, and college students. *Neuropsychology,* 18(2), 371–7.

Simmons, A. (2002). *The story factor: Inspiration, influence, and persuasion through the art of storytelling.* Cambridge, MA: Perseus.

Wallace, M. T., Ramachandran, R., & Stein, B.E. (2004). A revised view of sensory cortical parcellation. *Proceedings of the National Academy of Sciences (USA), 101(7),* 2167–72.

Webster, D. B. (1999). *Neuroscience of communication.* San Diego, CA: Singular Publishing Group, Inc.

Wiggins, G., & McTighe, J. (2005) *Understanding by design* (2nd ed.). Alexandria, Virginia: Association for Supervision and Curriculum Development.

Wilcox, L. (2007) Unpublished audiotaped interviews of college students learning language systems. Aurora, NE.

Young, R.V. (2007). The university possessed. *The intercollegiate review* (pp. 3–9). Wlmington, DE: Intercollegiate Studies Institute.

PART III

TECHNOLOGICAL CLASSROOM CLIMATES AS INCLUSIVE LEARNING COMMUNITIES

CHAPTER 7

TECHNOLOGY CONNECTING CURRICULUM, INSTRUCTION, AND ASSESSMENT

Mark C. Geary

KEY TERMS

Advanced Search; Content Producers; Digital Immigrants; Digital Natives; Technology Integration; Web Clicker; Web Collaboration Tools.

REFLECTIVE QUESTIONS

- How can instructors most efficiently utilize the vast array of technologies available to increase proficiency in technology within the discipline or profession?
- How does the technology classroom climate shift the role of students to content producers using instructional activities?
- How can instructors interconnect the curriculum to instruction and assessment using technology?

Teaching Inclusively in Higher Education, pages 115–133
Copyright © 2010 by Information Age Publishing
All rights of reproduction in any form reserved.

INTRODUCTION

Teaching in higher education is being transformed by technology (Zucker, 2008). As early as 1983, when the *Nation at Risk* report called for computer science as a core competency for young students, the country has been aware of the need for students and their instructors to understand the computer as an information, computation, and communication device; use the computer in the study of the other basics and for personal and work-related purposes; and understand the world of computers, electronics, and related technologies (*Nation at Risk*, 1983). That report was written well before the widespread use of the internet and personal computers, and the awareness that the need to be effective in the 21st century has included the need to integrate technology into all skill areas.

As the Partnership for 21st Century Skills advocates:

> To cope with the demands of the 21st century, people need to know more than core subjects. They need to know how to use their knowledge and skills—by thinking critically, applying knowledge to new situations, analyzing information, comprehending new ideas, communicating, collaborating, solving problems, making decisions. (2003, p. 9)

Instructors no longer focus on a single lesson to a single homogenous group of students, but rather a multitude of activities directed to diverse and sometimes distant learners (Nixon & Leftwich, 1998).

With increasingly diverse college classroom, *technology integration* is both a challenge and an opportunity. It is challenging to follow emerging technologies and integrate them into instruction, but there are affordances created by the technology integration that enables instructors to successfully teach students who would have been deemed unreachable a decade ago. Addressed elsewhere in the book are ways technology is transforming education through distributed learning systems. Still unanswered is the question of how college instructors can most effectively use technology to improve learning outcomes for their own content area. Is there truly "no significant difference," as Larry Cuban (2001) suggested, or is the time and effort involved learning how to use the technologies worth the effort?

In an era where colleges and universities are evaluated on their ability to graduate students whose academic standing may not have even permitted them to enroll a few years previously, the challenges are great for today's college instructors. Students cannot be counted on to read the chapter before coming to class and instructors cannot be assured that students even have the ability to understand the text when they do read it. Negotiating the complexities of the college environment may be particularly challenging for first generation college students and college students whose English is a second language.

Yet technology does suggest ways to reach out to create an inclusive classroom community. College instructors understand from Gardner (1983) that there are multiple intelligences at work, and instructors can draw from Burmark (2004) and Cavanaugh (2006) on ways in which instructors can use visual images to support learning (refer back to Ch. 6 for previous discussion). Instructors watch the self-propelled development of a learning center called YouTube advance and grow, almost of its own volition, and wonder how to turn the visual and entertainment value of YouTube and other video websites into a learning structure. Finally, inclusive college instructors watch and learn from the college students themselves.

The focus of this chapter will seek to establish uses of technology that college instructors can implement into their instruction without having to master complex programming. One of the key skills for the 21st century is for students to be *content producers* on the Internet and it behooves inclusive instructors to help students make that transition. While the technical tools may be new or unfamiliar, the effort will be made to increase the comfort level by tying the tools to pre-existing instructional strategies and theories. Students who utilize these tools can become competent content producers. Technology continually changes, evolves to needs and perceived needs. Teaching changes as well, but not at the same rate. When looking at what technologies to learn and incorporate into their teaching, instructors need to ask: "Do I have time to learn this? Is there time in my course to teach it to my students? Will my students take the necessary time to learn it well?" Sometimes, the answer an emphatic "No!" sometimes a softer "Not yet," and still other times, the answer is "Yes, the instructor needs to do something different." This chapter suggests highly-effective instructional strategies for using technology that are cognizant of the value of the instructor's most precious resource, time.

Inclusive college instructors will learn ways to use technology in different forms and formats that will enable the building of inclusive learning communities in their college classroom. Instructors will learn ways technology can assist in both formative and summative assessment, while both learning from and teaching their students in various aspects of technologies. When it comes to technology, inclusive instructors may find the following quote helpful: "We teach best that which we most need to learn. We are all teachers, learners, and doers together" (Bach, 1977).

SHIFT IN INSTRUCTORS' ROLE

A frequently-heard phrase is "kids today." It is usually followed by some disparaging remark, like "Kids today don't know how to do real work" or "Kids today cannot listen for five minutes." While the relative truth of these assertions may vary widely, and is frequently disproven by actual studies, it is true that many of today's students have grown up in a significantly different environment than their college instructors. This point can be illustrated through the following example.

While giving a test review for the final exam in one college course, the college instructor decided to use a Jeopardy game review to facilitate involvement. The instructor let the winning team get three extra points on the exam. The top students earning an A had already been released to do a short essay activity. At the end of fifteen questions, the instructor explained that the game was over, as the remaining 10 questions were obscure humorists of the 19th century, left over on the template from a previous activity in another class. "You won't know any of those answers," the instructor asserted. The students asked if they could use their laptops to help find the answers. The instructor said they could, but would be limited to the thirty second timeframe used in the Jeopardy game. To the instructor's stunned surprise, the students got every answer correct.

When the college instructor recovered from being stunned, experience required intense reflection. How was the instructor using the Internet in the class example above? College students can be excellent researchers. Even when they may not know the answer to a specific content focused question, they can find the answer whenever they are connected to the Internet. What content was truly important, if they could research virtually anything in thirty seconds? What experiences could the instructor give the class that would aid them in becoming better students? For this course, the partial answer was to develop activities that encouraged, pushed even, the students to view life situations from different perspectives. This chapter will discuss ways of integrating technology while becoming more inclusive in the college classroom.

WEB SEARCHES

Prensky (2001) is acknowledged to have coined the term *digital natives*. While the use of the phrase has been somewhat controversial, the term is meant to distinguish between those who have always grown up in a digitally immersed environment, with easy access and high comfort levels of using computers, the internet, and other digital devices from *digital immigrants* (See ch. 9 for further discussion). The term digital native draws an analogy to a country's natives, for whom the local religion, language, and folkways are natural and indigenous, over immigrants to a country who often are expected to adapt and assimilate to their newly adopted home. Prensky (2001) implies that the youth of today can do anything requiring computers proficiently and effectively. Intuitively, this idea makes sense, but in actual research, usability studies say otherwise (Nielsen, 2005b). The Nielsen study refuted teen stereotypes. Teens are not in fact super Web geniuses who can use anything a website throws at them. In the Nielsen study, the measured a success rate was only 55% for the teenage users, which was substantially lower than the 66% success rate found for adult users in a broad test of a wide range of websites. The success rate indicates the proportion of times users were able to complete a representative and perfectly feasible task on the target site. This indicates the need to consider broader data sources before reaching conclusions about what today's students can and cannot do.

According to the Nielsen study (2005b), teens' poor performance is caused by three factors: insufficient reading skills, less sophisticated research strategies, and a dramatically lower patience level. Inclusive college instructors must teach their college students to understand and use *advanced search* techniques. Advanced searches require knowledge of the content and the quality of curiosity to guide the searches. Instructors frequently work to create a more equitable learning environment in which increased proficiency with technology is an outcome for college students. They need to help students who may have grown up with little or no Internet access succeed in that medium. Thus, inclusive college instructors become facilitators of the development of students' proficiencies.

While many instructors may be uncomfortable using websites, most are familiar with doing some research in the library using the computer card catalogue, and understand the three cornerstones of Boolean search, "and", "or," and "not." An example may be useful here. Suppose the college instructor wanted to look up wild mustangs in the west. The instructor could search for "mustang," but would return several thousand results for the car, the Ford mustang. Even if the instructor added "and horses," the instructor still might have lots of Ford mustang results, as "horses" frequently is used for "horsepower." However, if the instructor searched Google for "mustang and horses –Ford" (the minus sign is how Google represents "not"), the instructor still has over a million results, but virtually all of the car results have been eliminated. To be still more specific, if the instructor searches for "wild mustang in the west" using quotation marks to get that exact phrase, the instructor would have only eight results, but three are very relevant. By using these four search tools, "and," "or," "not" (minus, on Google) and "quotes" the college instructor is able to create a refined search that helps get the information needed. To make this even simpler, the college instructor and students should learn to set the advanced search on Google as the homepage on their web browser, instead of the basic search page. Students will find the advanced search features spelled out in the advanced page. More information is available at: http://www.google.com/educators/.

SEARCH USING CELL PHONES

As noted earlier, students' struggles on the web stemmed from three factors: insufficient reading skills, less sophisticated research strategies, and a dramatically lower patience level. Some search skills were addressed in the previous section, but how does the inclusive college instructor help students with literacy needs (Nielsen, 2005a) become more proficient readers and writers? There are no simple solutions, but Vygotsky (1978) offers a partial solution with the concept of scaffolding. Inclusive college instructors enhance scaffolding opportunities by reducing the complexity of the material into smaller, more discrete segments, which are compatible with existing student schema.

From a technological perspective, one of the tools college students use most frequently is the text messaging function on their cell phone. By combining the physical feature of their cell phone with the virtual features of Google Simple Messaging Service (SMS), college students can increase the amount of non-fiction reading they do through SMS search, while exercising their advanced search skills. Google SMS can be used to find restaurants, check the weather, get directions, and get sports scores. Perhaps most importantly, SMS has a glossary which allows students to look up words and ideas. Students who would not be caught dead using a dictionary do not hesitate to look up words on their cell phone. This is an example of a new, but growing field of mobile learning (mLearning) through the medium of cell phones (Geary, 2008). For example, a student could text "define star" to 466453 (the number used to text message Google) and have the astronomical definition of a star returned. This in turn can lead to further classroom discussion.

In the course of implementing technological solutions, it is important that inclusive college instructors do not duplicate poor instructional strategies that have been used in the past (Beers, 2003). This means that rather than using Google SMS as a dictionary, the students are better served using it as a thesaurus, looking at the similar words given, discussing them with a partner, examining the context they are used in, and developing a definition that fits for them while conveying the meaning. Technology can enhance class interaction and should not be used as a substitute for it.

Inclusive instructors can facilitate the use of cell phones as search tools by asking students to look up a term or set of terms that has a meaningful, but not necessarily precise connection to the material being taught. Then students are grouped to discuss the terms. If different groups were given different terms, they could each report back out on what they found. In an education course, an instructor might have one set of students search democracy, another group search repression, and another search freedom. The groups would be given five minutes to review the results Google SMS sends to their cell phones, create a definition in their own words, and explain how their search relates to education. Two of the tools that instructors are likely find useful are glossary and question and answer (Q&A). These two tools allow a wide range of options for instructors, including the thesaurus activity mentioned above and developing questions based on the content being delivered. Inclusive college instructors can send a text message like "glossary freedom" or "Q&A Abraham Lincoln birthday to 466453." Instructors can find more information at: http://www.google.com/mobile/products/sms.html#p=default

VISUAL STRATEGIES ENABLED BY TECHNOLOGY

Being able to visualize the material being learned is a key skill (Marzano, Pickering, & Pollack, 2001; Tovani, 2004). Inclusive college instructors can enhance that skill by creating concept maps of their own courses, to help students form a schema (refer back to Ch. 4 for previous discussion) of what is being learned while helping the inclusive instructors organize how they are going to teach it. With the expanding popularity of Web 2.0 tools (see Ch. 9 for further discussion) inclusive instructors find it easier to create and share concept maps than ever before. In addition, instructors can ask their students to create concept maps to get an idea of what they already know about a given topic, or what they have learned or remembered. Concept maps then become a mirror for reflecting students' thoughts, and can be used at almost any point in the course.

In order to use a concept map, inclusive college instructors can utilize a tool like Bubbl.us, or a free software download, like cmaptools to create online and digital graphic organizers. While Inspiration concept mapping software (www.inspiration.com) has some advantages, the cost over the free alternatives makes it a secondary choice for many college instructors, especially if they are asking students to participate in the concept map creation process using digital tools. There are many concept mapping tools available for free. However, Bubbl.us is preferred for ease of use by many and cmaptools is favored for the robust feature set (see Figure 7.1).

The Bubbl.us tool is well known for the ease of use and any content can work. The menu is inconspicuous, but very important. From the Menu, college students can export the concept map as a graphic.jpg image, or export it as an outline in html format. When exported as an html outline, the graphic becomes the start of an outline that can be used for notes, or writing prompts (see Figure 7.2).

Cmaptools is a software program created by the University of West Florida, Central Florida, and the IHMC. It is free for college instructors and college students, frequently updated and has all the common concept map

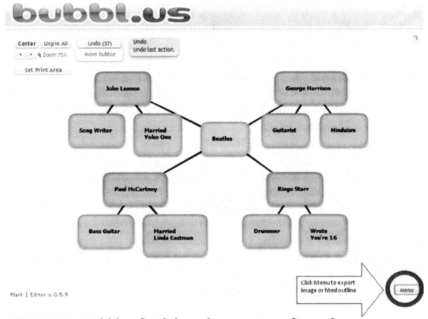

FIGURE 7.1. Bubbl.us [Web-based computer software].
Retrieved November 24, 2009, from http://bubbl.us/

creation features It also has the ability to help college students generate a portfolio of their digital products online and the ability to search for other concept maps in the instructors, or students, area of interest online.

As college instructors plan their lessons, they need to examine the final goals and objectives of the lessons, as well as the instructional strategies used in the lessons, and the evaluation of the goals and objectives of the lessons. By using the visual tools, inclusive instructors are forced to visually organize the sequencing of the lesson to maximize student learning. It becomes easier for inclusive instructors to organize, deliver, and assess the content necessary to meet their course objectives. A tool like Bubbl.us can also be used as a pre and post assessment tool. Students can share a template online with other college students that they can expand into a more developed concept map. This map shows where their knowledge has grown from the beginning, or what knowledge they bring into the classroom.

The inclusive instructor provides the students with a partially constructed concept map in Bubbl.us. The inclusive instructor then shares the map with the students by entering the students' emails or account ID into the Bubbl.us friends section. The shared concept map can be distributed via

I.   Beatles

- **Beatles**
  - **John Lennon**
    - *Song Writer*
    - *Married*
      Yoko Ono
  - **Paul McCartney**
    - *Bass Guitar*
    - *Married*
      Linda Eastman
  - **Ringo Starr**
    - *Drummer*
    - *Wrote*
      You're 16
  - **George Harrison**
    - *Guitarist*
    - *Hinduism*

FIGURE 7.2.   Bubbl.us [Web-based computer software].

Retrieved November 24, 2009, from http://bubbl.us/._The Bubbl.us outline can be copy/ pasted into Word or another word Processing program, and used as a notes organizer or writing prompt. There is a plain option for the html export, but using colors is more engaging and provides visual cues for organization of writing. Bubbl.us concept maps can be saved online, shared, sent to an email account, and embedded on a webpage.

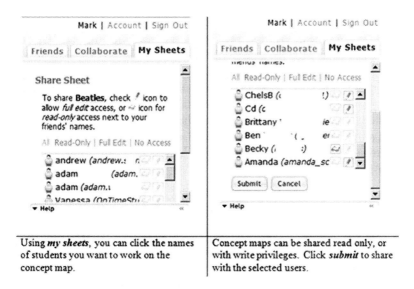

Using *my sheets*, you can click the names of students you want to work on the concept map.	Concept maps can be shared read only, or with write privileges. Click *submit* to share with the selected users.

FIGURE 7.3.   Bubbl.us [Web-based computer software].

Retrieved November 24, 2009, from http://bubbl.us/

the online sharing collaborate feature. Then the instructor can ask the students to create an additional twenty concepts related to the first four or five the instructor had given them. The shared concept map will appear under the collaborate tab under whatever name the student gives it. Instructors and students should use some combination of course name, assignment name and user name. As a fill-in-the-blank test, this is a difficult assignment for college students, but as a concept map, students seldom have difficulty in coming up with twenty related sub-concepts.

Inclusive college instructors can extend this by starting with the concept map and ask students to create a video from photos, further elaborating on the concept. While many students do not like writing term papers, the visual process and focus on digital images over words help students to engage with virtually any content from math to psychology. Concept maps can be used to demonstrate content knowledge through their inclusion in students' videos. Videos are frequently used by college students to obtain information, and concept maps help provide structure to their learning, both as they create the video, and as other students interact with the created works.

Photostory 3 is an ideal tool for use with digital concept maps. Other online photo sharing websites like Flickr.com and Photobucket.com offer a plethora of photographs that students can use copyright free. For PC users, free software such as Photostory 3, can help college students make videos out of their pictures. The students simply import their pictures, arrange them in the order they want to explain a concept, narrate picture by individual picture, add or have the program generate music, and create a movie that will play in Windows Media Player. Students import the graphic Jpeg images (.jpg file) created in Bubbl.us to a specific section. Students then move the images from the specific section of the Photostory 3 to the overall concept section of video. This builds into the video the long term memory (refer back to Ch. 6 for previous discussion). This can be repeated as needed, but ideally these types of digital videos tend to be between two and six minutes, with six minutes being the outer limit of the software. One caveat with adding music on a narrated video is making sure the narration is inaudible.

FACILITATING STUDENT ENGAGEMENT

Once students are familiar with making short videos from Photostories, these projects make a good replacement for the term paper. Such projects are useful in developing students' skills in *web collaboration tools*. One example is a project called blended video or sometimes Movie Mashups. Students must take three types of video: Photostory movies they have created,

YouTube clips they have downloaded (through Zamzar.com), and personal video. The students then blend, or re-mix the video using Windows Movie Maker 2 or Adobe Premiere Elements to create four to eight minutes of video describing key concepts. Such videos may require web collaboration tools to convey the illustrated concepts.

One example of a blended video was completed in a psychology class. Students did a video project to describe educational theorists. Previous results were poorly re-written papers or almost direct copies of papers that were out on the web. By making students re-conceptualize their individual understanding of their theorist through video and concept maps, the final products were much more cohesive and better produced. They are constructing their own knowledge, literally from the media which surrounds them. Inclusive instructors can adopt this procedure to almost any content area. This enables students to engage in rich media exploration of the topic in a visual format, using web collaboration tools for deeper learning. Another use of the Photostory video is to ask the students to create a brief one or two minute introduction of themselves. In this activity, students are sharing their hobbies, interests and what they hoped to get out of the class. The Photostory movie may be posted to online discussion boards for the class and the instructor to see.

Focusing on desired instructional outcomes is essential for using this technology for inclusive instruction in a meaningful way. Proficiency in the use of technology is a desirable by-product of the frequent and integrated use of technologies in the instructional setting. Inclusive instructors can improve student commitment to the video project by requiring that they be videotaped as part of the project. By creating intermediary steps, instructors can insure that the project is not done at the last minute, and that students will be successful, at least to the degree they follow the feedback given at each checkpoint/grading point. The learning curve needed to learn the technology such as MovieMaker 2 is about 30 minutes for most students. There can, however, be problems with individual video cameras. As inclusive instructors plan to use video technology, they need to prepare carefully to have the required components integrate seamlessly. They need to make sure digital camcorder cameras either have firewire export or have the original CD with drivers that came with them.

ASSESSMENT USING TECHNOLOGY

College instructors can focus their use of technology for assessment purposes in a meaningful way, including the technical requirements for the course in the syllabus. With training and research, it is possible to find a formalized process for proceeding. An example of this for online courses (and some face-to-face) is the Quality Matters rubric, where instructors can assess their course against suggested guidelines and rubrics created for online course review. Many of these guidelines apply equally well to face-to-face courses. Quality Matters emphasizes the importance of stating explicitly the objective and assessment for every assignment, and provides rubrics to gauge implementation.

Rubrics

What college instructors may think of as students complaining about assignments being hard may actually be students complaining about assignments being unclear, and the Quality Matters rubric helps clarify the requirements, both for instructors and students. For example, Quality Matters will ask if there is a digital game or online simulation that a student can use to prepare for a summative assessment. When college students know exactly what to do, why they were doing it, and how they were being assessed, they are less likely to be frustrated by the challenges of the course. This helps build a more inclusive classroom setting that invites participation from students operating at very different levels. As instructors improve the assignments to incorporate the Quality Matters guidelines, such as having an objective and an assessment attached to each assignment, student evaluation scores may rise as well.

Just as the Quality Matters rubric provides a useful guide to college instructors, many technology projects benefit from the implementation of rubrics to guide the students and assist the instructors in assessment. One extraordinarily valuable tool is Rubistar (rubistar.4teachers.org). This website provides excellent suggested rubric guides that can then be edited to meet specific course needs, and then shared as a permanent webpage that instructors and their students can link to. If instructors have uncertainty about how to develop a rubric, they can pick the most important criteria categories, then get some help from students. This can be done by taking a category, discussing with the students what would an outstanding project look like, and then working towards the middle from each side, usually creating a rubric that has three or four levels for each standard needed to evaluate the students. In Rubistar, it is important to save changes, save as a webpage when complete, and test the link. Besides giving the students a rubric, instructors can grade the project in multiple steps:

- Select topic;
- Create concept map/storyboard of what is going to be covered;
- Complete a rough draft movie; and
- Complete a final project.

Web Surveys

One technological tool, web surveys, has been a useful tool at the beginning of a course. SurveyMonkey is a free web survey, asking students two basic questions: What are your expectations coming into this course? What is your comfort level with the following technology tools? These questions inform the inclusive instructor of the college students' goals and needs. The students know that their college instructor cares where they are in their development. Certainly the best of the inclusive college instructors are those that made a personal connection to their students. While many people fear that technology will put a barrier between humans' ability to relate to others, technology such as this may bring us closer together.

The response of the college students to survey questions can be varied and sometimes startling. College instructors may ask students to answer anonymously to questions that would be uncomfortable for them to answer directly. Questions can be oriented towards understanding of a concept, such as: How well do you understand X at this point in the course? Other questions could be recall based and might take the place of a pop quiz, but can provide the college instructor with valuable information. These tools are a great opportunity to get to know college students without being invasive of their privacy or damaging to their self-esteem. By giving students multiple and, occasionally, anonymous inputs into the class, college instructors build a more inclusive classroom setting. College instructors will have multiple formative assessment opportunities that will enable course modifications, better serving students' needs.

Clickers

One set of technological tools in college classrooms is clickers. They are electronic laser devices that let students anonymously answer from a predetermined select range of choices. Most interactive whiteboards on the market today have clickers. They provide students with the ability to respond to questions posted on Power Point slides. They also allow the instructor to maintain control of the flow of the class while making the class more interactive for students. There can be some difficulties in locating sufficient numbers of them, making sure all batteries are charged, and ensuring that the students know how to work them.

What can work quite well in inclusive college classrooms is the *web clicker* concept applied to cell phones (Geary, 2008). This is made possible, not just through new cell phone capabilities, but through improved applications to support cell phones. One such application is a website, called PollEvery-Where (www.PollEveryWhere.com). This application allows the inclusive instructor to create an online, anonymous poll that students can answer via text message (SMS), twitter, or on the website. This has the effect of making cell phones into web clickers. The web clickers interact with a remote website via text message, thus allowing more student activity within the class.

BUILDING ELECTRONIC GROUPS

Just as live classroom discussion groups add richness to the instructional environment, the electronic tools available over the Internet allow that richness to incur with more diverse participation of the students. College students who might hesitate to participate in a live classroom discussion are frequently more engaged in the electronic environment. Many, if not most, of the goals of 21st century skills could be summarized as create, collaborate, and communicate. Fortunately, this is an era when technological tools are ubiquitous, allowing these goals to be achieved. For example, Google now has online spreadsheets and word-type applications that allow users to share documents almost simultaneously across the web, with robust commenting features that allow for college instructors' critique. What this means for inclusive instructors is that electronic group projects become easier to incorporate into the college course. However, inclusive instructors need to track the group process carefully. It also means that college students should be graded on their contribution to the process, what they are actually learning, and how they work through the group process.

At the time of this writing, Google did not have an equivalent to Power Point, although it was rumored to be coming soon. There are two sites, www.slideshare.com and www.voicethread.com, that are quite well suited for sharing Power Point slides and can be useful for creating a finished group online project. Similar to Google Docs, Buzzword Acrobat (www.buzzword.acrobat.com) allows for shared documents, just as Google Docs does, but has a much more intuitive commenting feature. This allows comments to stay out to the side of the document like Word, rather than embedding the comments in the lines of text, like Google Docs does. Students could create and share a Buzzword document that has the storyboard built into it using the tables feature and share the completed video using Adobe share website. Peer commenting could be enabled through the use of these tools by giving classmates access to the video files. Combined, these tools create a useful home base for group projects where documents can be easily shared, instructor feedback freely given, and final products of the group project disseminated. Electronic group projects of this type allow college students and instructors a broader range of technological opportunities to enhance instruction and build inclusiveness in the college classroom.

USING ELECTRONIC GAMES

Many students today come to college already proficient in electronic games. However, college instructors have not readily used electronic games in the classroom setting to teach either academic content or concepts. Some thought should be given by inclusive college instructors on how to moderate games for maximum student involvement. Some college instructors prefer working in groups of three, or even five, to keep more students involved at any given time. The instructor can also rotate which students can respond on a team each turn. Inclusive instructors will have to find what works best for them. A few key ideas to remember will be helpful for any game:

- Extrapolate the learning from the game being played.
- Take advantage of the visual nature of the game to clarify difficult or obscure references in your course text.
- There are usually multiple levels, so that while the first level the game demonstrates may be too basic for a college level class, the instructor can quickly scaffold to the level appropriate for student challenge and success.

Content Specific Games

For games specific to content areas, inclusive instructors will need to conduct an Internet search. If teaching physics for example, the websites www.physicsgames.net and www.flashphysicsgames.com can provide college instructors with more focused options for games designed specifically for content in physics. However, a simple Google search for "Physics" and "games" results in 22.5 million results. To use another example, college history instructors might wish to consider using the Muzzy Lane software, *Making History.* To quote from their website:

> MAKING HISTORY® is a series of award-winning counterfactual turn-based strategy games that place players into the role of world leader at a time of economic strife, conflicting ideologies, and looming threat of war. Players find themselves in a detailed, unpredictable world that reacts to their choices.... With each turn, players experience the tension and anticipation of seeing if their best laid plans will succeed, or lead their nation to ruin. (MuzzyLane.com, 2009)

In short, college students get to experience history as a world leader. What better way to bring history to life? This robust activity has proven to be an engaging alternative and supplement to textbook and lecture-based learning.

Many possibilities exist in multiple fields from sociology and psychology to literature and writing courses. Somewhat similar software is A Force More Powerful—The Game of Nonviolent Strategy (2005), a simulation tool for teaching non-violent conflict resolution. This game is an interactive teaching tool built on nonviolent strategies and tactics historically used successfully in conflicts around the world. The game simulates nonviolent struggles to win freedom and secure human rights against dictators, occupiers, colonizers, and corrupt regimes, as well as campaigns for political and human rights for minorities and women. It models real-world experience, allowing players to devise strategies, apply tactics and see the results. Implementing the technologically advanced content specific games into the college classroom increases student engagement and involvement with other students and with the content being taught.

Classroom-Mediated Games

In addition to content specific games, which can be quite elaborate and very professionally developed, there are also classroom-mediated games that replicate common games shows like Jeopardy or Who wants to be a Millionaire? Since these games are freely available on the web as Power Point templates, all the inclusive instructor has to do is come up with fill-in-the-blank-questions. Answering Jeopardy questions may result in factual recall or the beginning levels of Bloom Taxonomy. However, when inclusive instructors allow college students to create the questions, higher levels of thinking such as synthesizing or evaluating may occur.

Content Independent Games

In addition to classroom mediated games and content specific games, there are also content independent games that allow college instructors to place their content on the web, with little or no technological experience. Class Tools (www. ClassTools.net, 2009) allows inclusive instructors to create arcade games in their content areas. Instructors need to have between 10 and 25 matching questions, with the term and definition separated by an asterisk (but on the same line). Students can then go to the saved url, and select from one of several arcade games to play the content independent game. The better the college students know the content, the more successful they will be. Key instructor tips for this tool are to save the html file, provide a password to prevent student tampering, and remember to copy and paste the public url. Forgetting to do so can make it difficult to get back to the quiz.

CONCLUSIONS

This chapter has provided a foundation in technology integration from which inclusive college instructors can develop engaging instructional experiences. The activities selected are designed for maximum instructional gain and student interactivity, while minimizing the time needed to implement them. Today's inclusive instructors must incorporate technology into the learning process to enable increased engagement and learning from all students. The use of instructional strategies that incorporate technology will have both classroom and global benefits. Which technologies are implemented and in what order are professional decisions based on instructors' comfort level with technology, the time available to learn new techniques, and on willingness to learn.

Inclusive college instructors allow their students to teach as well as learn. In a society with a rapid pace of change, inclusive instructors must be engaged learners. Even if an instructor's content area is not rapidly changing, the methods and opportunities for sharing and teaching the content area are changing. The question is what inclusive college instructors want to learn and what channels are best suited to learning. Careful consideration should be given to changes in college courses, such as which blogs are added to Google Reader. For example, some blogs will be multiple tutorials, with little cognitive situating done, some blogs will be simply a listing of the latest websites available to accomplish a specified instructional task, and some websites provide an overview on what is happening in the world of instructional technology. Focusing too narrowly in any single area can be self-limiting. However, too broad of a focus is overwhelming. Carefully matching time available to implement the instructional technologies with the tools that will provide the greatest impact for students is the best course of action for inclusive college instructors.

REFERENCES

Bach, R. (1977). *Illusions*. New York: Delacorte Press/Eleanor Friede

Beers, K. (2003). *Why kids can't read*. Portsmouth, NH: Heinemann.

Bubbl.us [Web-based computer software]. Retrieved from http://bubbl.us/

Burmark, L. (2004). *Visual literacy*. Alexandria, VA: Association for Supervision and Curriculum Development.

BuzzWord [Web-based computer software]. Retrieved from https://buzzword.acrobat.com/

Cavanugh, C. (2006). *Clips from the classroom: Learning with technology DVD and activity guide.* Upper Saddle River, NJ: Prentice-Hall.

ClassTools.Net. [Web-Based computer software] Retrieved from http://classtools.net/education-games-php/quiz/

Cmap Tools. [Computer Software] Retrieved from http://cmap.ihmc.us/concept-map.html

Cuban, L. (2001). *Oversold and underused: Computers in the classroom.* Cambridge, MA: Harvard University Press.

Flickr.com. [Web-Based computer software] Retrieved from http://www.flickr.com/

A Force more Powerful: The game of nonviolent strategy. (2005). [Computer Software] York Zimmerman. Retrieved from http://www.aforcemorepowerful.org/game/index.php

Gardner, H. (1983). *Frames of mind.* New York, NY: Basic Books.

Geary, M. (2008). Supporting cell phone use in the classroom. *Florida Educational Leadership, 9*(1), 29–32.

Marzano, R. J., Pickering, D. J. & Pollack, J. E. (2001). *Classroom instruction that works: Research based strategies for improving student achievement.* Alexandria, VA: Association for Supervision and Curriculum Development.

Muzzy Lane Software. (2009). [Computer Software] *Making History.* Retrieved from http://www.muzzylane.com/ml/making_history

Nation at Risk. (1983) Retrieved from http://www.ed.gov/pubs/NatAtRisk/recomm.html

Nielsen, J. (2005a). Low literacy users. *Alertbox,.* Retrieved from http://www.useit.com/alertbox/20050314.html

Nielsen, J. (2005b). Usability of websites for teenagers. *Alertbox,.* Retrieved from http://www.useit.com/alertbox/teenagers.html

Nixon, M., & Leftwich, B. R. (1998). Leading the transition from the traditional classroom to a distance learning environment. *T.H.E. Journal, 26*(1), 54–57.

Partnership for 21st Century Skills. (2003). *Learning for the 21st century.* Retrieved from http://www.21stcenturyskills.org

Photobucket.com. [Web-Based Computer Software] Retrieved from http://photobucket.com/

Photostory 3. (2006) [Computer Software]. Redmond, WA: Microsoft.

PollEveryWhere.com [Web-Based Computer Software] Retrieved from http://www.polleverywhere.com/

Prensky, M. (2001). Digital natives, digital immigrants. *On the Horizon, 9*(5), 1–2. Retrieved from http://www.marcprensky.com/writing/Prensky%20-%20Digital%20Natives,%20Digital%20Immigrants%20-%20Part1.pdf

Quality Matters Online course Rubric Retrieved from http://qminstitute.org/home/Public%20Library/About%20QM/RubricStandards2008-2010.pdf

Rubistar.4teachers.org [Web-Based Computer Software] Retrieved from http://rubistar.4teachers.org/

Survey Monkey. [Web-Based Computer Software] Retrieved from http://www.surveymonkey.com/

Tovani, C. (2004). *Do I really have to teach reading?* Portland, ME: Stenhouse Publishing Co.

Voice Thread. [Web-Based Computer Software] Retrieved from http://voicethread. com/#home

Vygotsky, L. (1978). *Mind in society.* Cambridge, MA: MIT Press.

Zucker, A. (2008). *Transforming schools with technology: How the smart use of digital tools helps achieve six key education goals.* Cambridge, MA: Harvard University Press.

CHAPTER 8

REACHING STUDENTS THROUGH A VIRTUAL COMMUNITY

**Shelley B. Harris, Jennifer C. Wilson, and
Jacqueline M. Ferguson**

KEY TERMS

Asynchrony; Hybrid Course; Self Efficacy; Student Centered Learning Environments; Synchrony; Virtual Learning Community.

REFLECTIVE QUESTIONS:

- What is a virtual learning community and how can it impact students' self-efficacy?
- How can virtual communities reach diverse college students and provide a student-centered learning environment?
- How are virtual communities utilized in the classroom to promote student success through tools such as asynchronous and synchronous chat or hybrid courses?

Teaching Inclusively in Higher Education, pages 135–154
Copyright © 2010 by Information Age Publishing
All rights of reproduction in any form reserved.

OVERVIEW

We are in the midst of one of the most dramatic technological revolutions in history. As such, education is evolving to meet the demands of a global society (Leu, 2001; Reinking & Bridwell-Bowles, 1991). College instructors need to cultivate a variety of literacies within students to provide them with a competitive, economic edge. Colleges and universities act as a cultural bridge to those new literacies empowering individuals and groups traditionally excluded from education thereby reconstructing the classroom to make it responsive to the challenges of an ever-changing society. Using technological tools to create and extend *virtual learning communities* requires that instructors embrace the concept of new instructional strategies to enhance traditional educational experiences. This chapter will discuss the foundational underpinnings of building a virtual learning community and develop a framework of establishing a virtual community system in the higher education classroom by using technology as a tool to reach all students and embrace the 21st century.

DEFINING VIRTUAL LEARNING COMMUNITIES

Establishing an effective classroom community is paramount in promoting success in the diverse college classroom. Inclusive college instructors design classroom communities to offer all students an opportunity for creating meaning in what they are learning and to institute authorship for that learning (Rushkoff, 2004). Many learning theorists, such as Glasser (1993) and Noddings (2006), contend that a classroom is defined as its own inclusive community and serves students best when safe, predictable routines and procedures are established.

Within the field of education, time and money are allocated to the designs of classrooms that make these communities inviting to all students. Instructional choices should focus on meeting the unique needs of all students in the hope to facilitate their overall success within the inclusive community. The idea of using technology to facilitate the creation and maintenance of such learning communities is an emerging and growing field of research in virtual learning communities. Although relatively new and viewed upon as a separate aspect to teaching and learning, an online component to a classroom does not have to hinder the established sense of community. In fact, it can strengthen community by including an additional modality to learning, thus addressing more diverse student needs. As with any traditional organization of classrooms, the establishment of effective procedures and expectations to integrate students into a virtual learning community is essential.

In addition to community building practices, social learning (Bandura, 1977) and constructivism (Vygotsky, 1978) are dependent aspects of a virtual learning community. Both theories suggest that learning takes place in a social environment and that through this exploration, meaning is obtained. Actively constructing one's knowledge can occur through the use of effective instructional decisions and establishing protocol for the network of learners in a virtual learning community. By using various online elements, students are given additional resources to derive meaning. The larger the variety of classroom instruction, the more likely the diverse student needs will be met. As an inclusive community of practice (Lave & Wagner, 1990), students are able to conceptualize their learning by participating in a network of learners. Virtual learning communities are simply the same framework taken into a digital realm.

Such social learning theory proposes the importance of self-efficacy for understanding how instructors envision themselves as consumers in a virtual environment. *Self-efficacy* asserts that individuals who believe they have the skills or qualities that are necessary to ensure positive results manifest a sense of efficacy (Bandura, 1977). As it applies to the integration of technology and virtual learning environments, self-efficacy beliefs towards technology integration have been theorized to be a determining factor in each instructor's choice to utilize technology to improve teaching and learning (Wang, Ertmer, & Newby, 2004). This self-labeling as competent technology users (instructors or students) helps to ensure persistence in the face of disappointment and satisfaction with outcomes likely. The versatility of a virtual learning community allows its diverse members to experience self-efficacy with their learning. Self-efficacy is the belief in one's abilities to excel within a particular domain (Bandura, 1977). For some students, a virtual learning community provides the anonymity necessary to take risks with their learning that they wouldn't normally take in a traditional setting. On the other hand, students with experience in technology come to the community with a high level of self-efficacy for using virtual tools to further their education.

Berners-Lee (1989) developed the World Wide Web with the intent to establish a medium for individuals to communicate virtually. A virtual learning community is a place online where people come together to connect, converse, read and respond. It provides an opportunity for individuals who are geographically separated to participate in a virtual learning community without the cost or limitation of travel. Members of the virtual community can participate from anywhere in the world, given that they have access to the appropriate technology. Since its inception, this virtual community has taken on many forms such as blogs, web pages, visual media and discussion boards. It is important to note that a virtual community, while open to the global society, does require membership criteria making each community

TABLE 8.1. Instructor Resources

Virtual Learning Community Tools	Suggested Classroom Activity
Blog	Journaling, grand conversations, writing prompts, Reflections, Podcasts
Web Page	Biography, Webcasts
Visual Media	Slide shows, graphic art, videos
Discussion Board	Reader response
Wiki	Writing process, revising, editing
Simulations	Museums, observations, reenactments, Role Play
Chat rooms	Voice Chat, Dialogue Preparation
Instant Messaging	Purpose, language, audience, word choice
Texting	Syntax, Narrative used Text Speak, Emotions, Text Lingo

inclusive in nature. These forms will be discussed throughout the remainder of the chapter.

When working to establish and maintain virtual learning communities, it is imperative that issues such as curriculum and instruction be addressed to meet the needs of all students in the technological age of the 21st century. Due to the fact that virtual communities are easily accessible, they can contain students from various backgrounds and locations, thus broadening the opportunities for inclusion in education. The key to the success of virtual learning communities lies in deciphering the various types of online media and their relationship to educational instruction. The tools used to create and maintain effective virtual learning communities can be divided into two broad categories: asynchronous and synchronous. Within each of these categories is an array of tools available to enhance classroom instruction, meet the diverse needs of students, and create an inclusive classroom. Table 8.1 contains a list of tools and classroom activities as resources for instructors.

The remainder of this chapter will introduce these tools, provide examples of their function and state instructional ideas for creating an inclusive virtual community within the tools.

TOOLS FOR CREATING VIRTUAL LEARNING COMMUNITIES

Within the vastly expanding parameters of online communities, two forms, those of *asynchrony* and *synchrony*, permeate the landscape and dictate the type and approach taken in developing an inclusive virtual community.

Asynchrony discussion takes its definition from the fact that it is a meaning separate from synchrony, creating an educational environment without the limitations of real-time interaction. With this format, there may be a delay of hours or even days between a question, comment, or response. Technological platforms such as discussion boards and blogs act as examples of asynchronous discussion sites. While asynchrony calls for the passage of unmonitored amounts of time, synchronous tools offer discourse patterns that occur at the moment and in real time. Synchronous activities consist of real-time interaction between members of the community, regardless of the members' location. These types of activities often occur in a conversational pattern (one writes, another writes etc.). Examples of synchronous activities include online chats and simulations.

Tools within each category will be discussed further and detailed instructions on how each component can be used to create an inclusive virtual community will be outlined. It is also important to note that with technology continuing to evolve at an ever increasing pace, this chapter by no means contains an exhaustive list of tools for building an inclusive virtual community. Regardless of the mode, however, each new technological tool should be viewed and evaluated through a critical lens to determine its use for education.

Asynchronous Tools

Asynchronous tools are designed to deliver information in stagnant forms, which operates with no real-time factors. Such tools allow a community to stay in contact without the burden of meeting in the same location at the same time. Some examples discussed in this section include: blogs, social networking websites, visual media, and discussion boards.

Blogs

In the 21st century, many students use some sort of emailing, text messaging or MySpace page to communicate and express their thoughts. Blogging is equally as popular and can be utilized in the education profession to reach, motivate, and teach students. In its original design, blogging was intended to be a place where individuals could read and write their thoughts (Richardson, 2006). See Chapter 9 for more information on this topic. Mostly, individuals use this as a personal form of communication. However, including this form of media in the college classroom can allow for students to construct meaning about content and for inclusive instructors to facilitate the meta-cognitive process.

Eide (2005) shows that blogging can "promote critical thinking, be a powerful promoter of creative, intuitive, and associational thinking, promote analogical thinking, be a powerful medium for increasing access and exposure to quality information, and combine the best solitary reflection and social interaction" (pp. 1–2). In essence, blogs can appeal to both the intrapersonal and interpersonal learning styles of the students. To reiterate this point, Huffaker (2005) states that, "In the classroom, students can have a personal space to read and write alongside a communal one, where ideas are shared, questions are asked and answered, and social cohesion is developed" (p. 94).

Current research is examining the effectiveness of blogging as an instructional tool within the college classroom. One particular study's results indicate that:

> those instructional benefits that had the highest levels of agreement tended to focus on the concepts of reflection, application, and engagement, all of which are key elements to successful college teaching. Specifically, the blogging opportunity is seen as an element of a class that brings students back to the subject matter and engages them to the extent that they want to be involved in a manner that does not embarrass them."(Brescia & Miller, 2005, p. 50)

Additionally, another study stated that, "Blogs provide a multi-genre, multimedia writing space that can engage visually minded students and draw them into a different interaction with print text" (Kajder & Bull, 2003, p. 34). These studies reiterate the point that blogging can be an effective tool in the college classroom when implemented effectively.

Implementation of blogging to the college classroom can be quite simple and fun. There are many avenues to take when incorporating a blog. One way to have students sign up for blogs is for a computer specialist at the university to create web space, or a portal, for students and faculty to access. Another easy way is to sign up to many of the free blog sites offered online. Once a class blog is set up, it can be used for various writing prompts, continuing classroom discussions, or reflections from readings. Students are able to post to the blog with written text, pictures and/or video to relay their learned information. In addition, students can respond to other classmate's blogs, which allows for deeper transfer of learning. Using blogs in the classroom is an effective way to reach all college students, regardless of socio-economic status, language barrier, or technical savvy.

Social Networking Websites

One of the most popular activities on the Internet is to connect with others socially (Knobel & Lankshear, 2004). This type of service allows individuals to build virtual communities online, as well as share and communicate information. MacManus (2006) reports that a third of people online visited a social networking site. This number of people visiting one of the

FIGURE 8.1. http://twitter.com/coolcatteacher

top online social networks has grown by over 109%, and social networking sites are now close to eclipsing traffic to Google and Yahoo http://www. readwriteweb.com/archives/social_networks_vs_portals.php#). The idea of following other students' postings and creating postings' for peers to read and respond creates a virtual learning community.

Twitter (www.twitter.com) is essentially a webpage for individuals to post thoughts limited in length (See Figure 8.1). In the classroom, Twitter is similar to discussion threads. Students can post a response and wait for classmates or instructors to reply. It is not instantaneous and not correlated, meaning that responses may get confused with the topics since postings aren't threaded. Facilitation of the various threads and topics is needed to keep students on task by organizing each thread into specific categories, chapters, or themes. Twitter can also be used as a content test or even a class announcement. It allows for everyone to respond to a question, not just the students called on in the traditional classroom setting. Finally, it is a great platform to input important facts or information that was not given in class. This effective form of communication extends opportunities for conversations in the college classroom. Twitter is considered a sounding board for individuals to express their thoughts and viewpoints about current issues and trends. By integrating this social concept into the college classroom, students can express their thoughts and ideas, while building a sense of togetherness. Thus, it can allow for students to talk to one another, creating a sense of inclusion to the virtual learning community classroom.

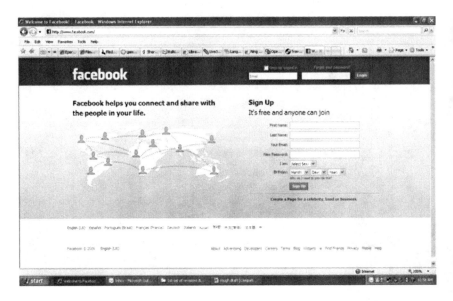

FIGURE 8.2.   http://www.facebook.com

Another example of a social networking website is Facebook. Facebook (www.facebook.com) is a place where students can post their profile, write daily musings, and maintain friendships (see Figure 8.2). It is a popular, free site that is used by all ages. Instructors can use this form of media to contact students, build a rapport with past and current students, as well as deliver instructional information. There are many strategies to use Facebook in the classroom. This is a great place to discuss group projects, take polls, and gather data. Also, students and instructors can offer feedback on lessons, ideas about content and even discuss various classroom management techniques. Easy access allows for instructors and students to go to the site at convenient times and post. Overall, student and instructor communication is increased and a commonality of community is formed beginning in the classroom and ending online. A detailed list of many social networking sites is outlined in Table 8.2.

Visual Media

Visual media is a form of online media that connects the individual with visual art such a videos and pictures. Two examples are Flickr (www.flickr.com), developed by Ludicorp and launched in 2004 as an online community program containing pictures and videos and You Tube (www.youtube.com). "People can see first-hand accounts of current events, find videos about their hobbies and interests, and discover the quirky and unusual" (http://www.crunchbase.com/company/youtube). There are many ways that visual media can be used in the classroom. Visual representations of information construct a multimodality approach to teaching and learning so that individual learning styles can be addressed. When presenting a difficult concept, using pictures or videos can increase the likelihood that students will better comprehend. Additionally, presentations are more interesting and can increase motivation in students. Visual media not just add to a lecture or presentation, but also can reiterate main ideas. Finally, integrating the visual arts actually enhances and encourages students' creativity.

Discussion Boards

Discussion boards are an excellent way to continue a discussion from a class or post new discussion topics. They are created on a server, either free standing or as part of the university. They are designed like email where someone will post a subject line and respond in the discussion area. Discussion boards are available to interested groups free of charge or part of course management system. Since they are online, accessibility is both easy and student/instructor friendly. Discussion boards can be utilized in the classroom in many different ways. First, it can be used to discuss main ideas or concepts that were introduced in the classroom. This extension of discussion allows for all college students to participate and for their voices to be heard. Also, discussion boards can be designed in such a way for students to correspond to each other on upcoming presentations or even ask questions about homework assignments. This is a great way for college students to communicate outside of the classroom and continue the dialogue about the course. Finally, discussion boards can be used to create and stimulate discussion among instructors and students, allowing for clarity of instructors' objectives and students' expectations. This form of communication can build rapport between inclusive college instructors and students.

Synchronous Tools

A limitation of asynchronous tools such as blogs, social networking websites, visual media and discussion boards, is that they can be stagnant; meaning that someone posts or uploads information and it remains by itself, without interaction. A solution to this dilemma may be to employ synchronous tools to create inclusive virtual learning communities. Such tools require an instantaneous response from the members of the community. Some examples discussed in this section include wikis, simulations, chat rooms, and instant messaging.

Wikis

Wikis (www.wikispaces.com) are a unique online format that, while providing information, allows members of the wiki to add to or delete the existing information. One facility currently utilizing wikis is the collaboration

TABLE 8.2. Sample Social Networking Sites

Name	Address	Description/Focus	Classroom Implementation
Amie Street	http://amiestreet.com/	Music – all genres	Incorporate music into a lesson, purchase or use free music in conjunction to writing, open a lesson with music
ANobii	http://www.anobii.com/	Books	Create an online bookshelf, review and rate books, organize books
Avatars United	http://www.avatarsunited.com/	Online simulation games	Create an avatar to represent current characters studied, simulates authentic situations
Blogster	http://www.blogster.com/	Spam-free blog cite, online journal, connect and share with classmates	Create writing samples to share online
Buzznet	http://www.buzznet.com	Photo, journal, video sharing community focusing on personal interests such a music, celebrities and media.	Create presentations or personal webpages with high interest topics
Care2	http://www.care2.com/	Green living and social activism	Create dialogue and language arts examples of social justice issues, debates, recipes
DailyBooth	http://dailybooth.com/	Photo-blogging site where users upload a photo every day	Create a personal memoir or daily journal. Daily opportunity to take photo, upload captions, and keep dialogue current.
DeviantART	http://www.deviantart.com/#	Art community	Incorporate art into lesson plans, presentations and in conjunction to literature and writing.
Epernicus	http://www.epernicus.com/	For research scientists	Learn about current scientific research, incorporate for experiments and essays
Facebook	http://www.facebook.com	Social webpage with pictures, videos, and comments about daily life	Create community in the classroom, respond to students comments, pose questions for students to answer

Site	URL	Description	Uses
Filmaffinity	http://www.filmaffinity.com/en/main.html	Movies and TV Series	Look at different points of view, create own advertisements for movies and TV, credibility, opinions
FledgeWing	http://www.fledgewing.com/	Entrepreneurial community targeted towards worldwide university students.	Create community with students, establish mentors and assistance
Flickr	http://www.flickr.com	Photo sharing, commenting, photography related networking, worldwide	Incorporate photos in a lesson, to open a lesson, or create own photo creation for fun
Goodreads	http://www.goodreads.com/	Library cataloging, book lovers	Read online books, recommend books to others, post reviews
italki.com	http://www.italki.com/	Language learning social network. 100+ languages.	Learn another language, build community in classroom by integrating other languages
LibraryThing	http://www.librarything.com/	Book lovers	Connect to others who read similar books, post and write about the books, compare and contrast opinions
LiveJournal	http://www.livejournal.com/	Blogging, journal, staying in touch	Build a classroom community with blogging and sharing information, pose questions to discuss
Livemocha	http://www.livemocha.com/	Online language learning - dynamic online courses in 22 languages - world's largest community of native language speakers.	Assist struggling or native English speakers in the class with visual, online learning
Ning	http://www.ning.com	Users create their own social websites and social networks	Create a classroom Ning to build community, share information, and keep in touch
Open Diary	http://www.opendiary.com/	First online blogging community, founded in 1998.	Blog information, keep a personal diary or journal, strengthens identity
TravBuddy.com	http://www.travbuddy.com/	Travel	Connects travelers going to same destinations, create in-class simulation of travel
Web-Biographies	http://www.webbiographies.com/	Genealogy and biography	Create a family tree, write your own memoir

http://en.wikipedia.org/wiki/Social_networking_sites

between the GILD, Texas A&M University—San Antonio, Alamo Community Colleges, and several other participating San Antonio Independent School districts. This project is known as the P-16 Blueprint for Success. Wikis are used as a source for information, gathering new and fresh ideas, and collaborating on what the stakeholders can do to increase college student success. One important factor to note is that wikis are not always considered reliable sources of information, since anyone can post to them. Therefore, when creating a wiki, certain parameters need to be in place. If used for learning purposes and in a controlled environment, they can be used for a variety of learning experiences where those involved know that the information they present is not only reliable but in a safe environment.

Wikis can be used in the classroom to create an online curriculum where college students will have an active role in participating (Richardson, 2006). This allows a sense of collaboration among students and college instructors, allowing instructors to customize each course. Second, wikis can be used as a personal collaboration among students in the classroom when conducting research. Being able to publish their findings online and compose together a collective piece of work can create motivation and self-efficacy among students. Since wikis are considered shared, this ongoing piece of writing can change form, be revised and edited, and show students how writing is a process and can be transformed. Wikis are a beneficial tool to use in the inclusive college classroom as it includes all students in the process of writing.

Simulations

Simulations are an effort to create a real world experience within an artificial setting (Borsook, 1997). In higher education, tools such as Second Life (Second Life Lab, 2003) can be used to create virtual communities that will mirror the real world. Some simulations are for pure enjoyment while others, when facilitated by a clear objective, are powerful learning tools. It is important to remember, however, that simulations are class manipulatives. They work best when the actual real world experience is not an option. Therefore, by using simulations, instructors are able to build prior knowledge of a specific concept or enhance a concept by adding to the instructional model. For example, biology students could use a simulation to explore the interdependency of organisms without disrupting the environment or traveling thousands of miles to view such an event first hand. The ability to play with the simulation powerfully brings the textbook facts to life. The military and medical fields are taking a lead in using simulations in their education programs (http://www.montgomerycollege.edu/ca/gaming, 2009). The military has flight, tank, and medial simulations to save the cost of equipment and human life. Medical simulations allow medical students to practice their knowledge prior to working with a live subject. Both of these examples allow more than one participant within the simulation, thereby creating a virtual community to practice and expand on their knowledge together.

Using computer simulations as out-of-class assignments (Ronen & Eliahu, 1999) offers students the opportunity to review concepts discussed in class. For example, science explorations may be difficult to complete at home due to a lack of proper equipment and/or supplies. An effective alternative is allowing students to complete the exploration virtually. After the students have explored the simulation, the inclusive instructor can debrief their understanding of the concept based on their new knowledge gained from the virtual experience, including how they worked together as a team in the operating room or the archeological excavation site. Business students may not be able to trade on the stock market while completing their degree, but can have the same experiences by virtually participating as a broker on Wall Street. History majors could have the ability to explore ancient civilizations through a simulation developed on Second Life (Foster, 2007), or software such as Sid Meier's Civilization (MicroProse, 1991), and Age of the Empires (MicroSoft, 1997). Within each of these simulations, students have the opportunity to create a virtual learning community that is no longer limited by the four walls of the classroom. Allowing students to participate in an authentic learning situation encourages a stronger connection to meaning making, thus resulting in overall knowledge retention. This is similar to project based learning, but is not limited to repeated costs and restrained locations, and it minimizes risk.

Chat Rooms

Chat rooms are virtual locations where individuals can sign in to simultaneously type their thoughts and respond to others' comments or questions. These designated locations allow inclusive college instructors and students to hold classroom discussions from various locations. Chat rooms involve individuals typing their ideas at the same time in an instant messaging format. It is, however, also possible for individuals to use webcams, allowing the participants to view and even hear one another in live time. There are also chat rooms available on the World Wide Web. These chat rooms are open to the public, but private chat rooms can also be created through platforms such as Yahoo or Windows Live. Private chat rooms created on the Internet require an invitation and specific log in to participate.

Once a chat room is designed, protocols explained, and specific log in time designated, chat rooms allow for an opportunity to build a virtual inclusive learning community wherein students can interact from anywhere that has Internet access. In order to facilitate such a discussion, the date, time and duration of each session should be published so as those participating can make proper arrangements for attendance. Since most chat sessions are text-based, meaning that people type their responses and others read, chat sessions should be limited to no more than ten students at a time to ensure optimal participation. Chat rooms can also be used to hold debates or book clubs and are not limited to only online courses. They can act as valuable tools that create space for students who process information differently (Schallert, Reed, & the D-Team, 2003–2004). When given the opportunity, students who may not be eager to speak in class or take on group leadership roles might find a chat room a comfortable way to share their ideas (Rowh, 2007).

The use of a synchronous chat room conversation has multiple positive aspects. It has the ability to accommodate students' personalities, while also honing their technological skills in academic and thoughtful ways. It is a way to create a space for all students to participate and also pushes those who are not as vocal in class to share. It allows time for thinking, as written language is often slower moving than oral speech. Also, a positive characteristic is that chat room discussion can quickly take on a life of its own, becoming a grand discussion, and providing a bit of anonymity for deep discussion and creating discourse. Participants can have multiple conversations at one time, even typing in conjunction with one another. Although this might make the text difficult to follow, a participating writer will become more facile with it over time.

To make the chat room experience productive, not only should a time and topic of discussion be coordinated and disseminated, but a facilitator should be present. This will help keep the discussion on track as well as insure all students are able to speak in their own time due to both technological needs and/or personality needs (Kittleson, 2002). This facilitator might ask particular students to respond, provide probing questions to require depth of thought and response, or clarify others' comments. Such chatiquette (ways of being a part of an online community) are important for creating a shared community. (see Ch. 9 for additional information). The participants must find a happy medium between structure and free conversation (Candler, Tucker, Triplett & Trautman, 2006). Too much structure and the ideas will be limited, often resulting in fewer comments. Having too much free conversation limits the objectives and curriculum of the course.

Messaging

Instant messaging (IM) is another component of a synchronous virtual community system. IM is typing a thought, comment or question to be posted on a network or the Internet for real time display. Instant message postings are used within chat rooms, email accounts such as Yahoo (www.yahoo.com) or Hotmail (www.hotmail.com) and popular social networking websites such as Facebook and My Space. The real time display mimics an actual conversation and separates this activity from asynchronous postings.

The process of responding in real time allows for immediate feedback; no more waiting three to five days for an answer from email.

Instant messaging is a good tool to use during virtual office hours. Sotillo (2003) contends that, according to her research, "IM is an ideal tool for learning, communicating, and community building" (p. 1). During virtual office hours with instant messaging, instructors can respond to multiple issues at one time without having to set up multiple appointments. Students who are unwilling to ask a question in class, may log on and present their concern, or pose questions they didn't know they had until they got home. By using IM, students are able to feel a personal, instant connection with their college instructors or other students, thus promoting a sense of an inclusive community.

Text messaging is similar to instant messaging in that they are both real time communications, but text messaging is used on a cellular phone network. Instructors can use texting to have students respond to a thought or question on Twitter, and then reply to each other (Rochman, 2009) instantaneously during a lecture. This process allows all students to give a response in real time. Text messaging is also an effective way to send students their homework assignments, remind them of important dates or tasks, and notify them quickly of any changes to the course schedule or content. Technology will continue to play a part in our social world, and we as educators should be seeking ways to engage and harness its uses for the benefit of all of our college students.

HYBRID COURSES

One current trend in higher education is the idea of a hybrid or blended class. *Hybrid courses*, according to Graham, Allen, and Ure (2003) are those that are offered using both the traditional face-to-face class time and an online component. Students will only meet about half the required class time in a face-to-face setting with the rest of the class time meeting online, conducting research or completing assignments. Growing numbers of students with varying needs have contributed to the popularity of hybrid courses (Anastasiades & Retalis, 2001). There are many challenges in designing a hybrid course successfully. "When designed carefully, a hybrid course combines the best features of in-class teaching with the best features of online learning to promote active student learning" (Garnham & Kaleta, 2002). Knowing ahead of time that they have two modes of classroom instruction, instructors can design lectures and activities in such a way to interest student participation and immediately set up a sense of community.

Each assignment in a hybrid course, regardless if it is face-to-face or online, should be meaningful and relate to the content of the course. Once

students recognize the value and integration of the online course requirements, greater participation will occur, thus resulting in establishing that
sense of an inclusive community. This delivery of instruction is not only
important for traditional teaching methods, but in imperative in designing
and establishing an inclusive virtual learning community. College students
must feel like they are a part of the process for true learning to occur.

Another challenge is setting up a direct and indirect line of communication with the students. This can be established through the use of technological tools such as e-mail, discussion boards, chat rooms, and discussion
threads designed for the purpose of communicating ideas, uploading written works, or posing grand conversations. Clear expectations and guidelines must be presented in order for students' comments to be meaningful and reflective. Some students may feel that there is disconnect when
online, but when there are many avenues to communicate, the doors to
establishing community will open. Inclusive college instructors play an active role in facilitating student online participation. Questions need to be
created ahead of time and be related to students and their learning. Inclusive instructors can also encourage "getting to know me" conversations
and postings. This, too, will permeate student involvement in the inclusive
classroom community.

Finally, the last challenge of hybrid courses is staying organized so that
students' frustration level is at a minimum. From the very beginning, there
is a strong need to make sure that computer systems are compatible and
what programs are used to operate. Limiting some of the basic frustrations
will allow college students to focus on the content and meaning of the concepts while at the same time becoming actively engaged in the online experience. Hybrid courses, as coined by many as the best of both worlds, are
designed in such a way to reach all students and meet their needs at the
university level.

Blackboard

As a result of an increased interest and necessity of using the Internet
as a tool to facilitate *student-centered learning environments*, online platforms
have been created to supplement traditional classroom instruction and aid
in the use of many of the asynchronous and synchronous tools discussed
above. Platforms allow an inclusive instructor to select which tools to use
and allow the creation and enhancement of inclusive virtual communities.
One such example of an online platform is Blackboard.

Blackboard is an online course management system that may be used
in full or partial accompaniment to face-to-face classroom time, thus creating features of a hybrid course. Blackboard allows the instructor to decide
which components to use in the classroom, whether to replace face-to-face
teaching in a physical classroom, partially replace face-to-face teaching,

or act solely as a supplement to existing face-to-face teaching (Arbaugh & Duray, 2002). In utilizing Blackboard, inclusive instructors seek to aid the achievement of learning outcomes through improved access to learning materials, the provision of more timely feedback to college.

One example of how Blackboard has had a positive effect on students is a study conducted by Jones and Lea (2008). Their study indicates that:

> Among those participants who embraced social networking, it became clear that they were engaged in multifaceted kinds of interactivity in which they took on different roles and constructed identities within the textual space of the interaction. The positioning that took place in the interactions enabled them to cultivate friendship and camaraderie whilst also doing work for university assignments. (p. 21)

By implementing Blackboard or another online course management system, the focus can change from an instructor-directed atmosphere to a student-centered and student-led environment. Therefore, the learning generated from the discussions can be more meaningful and personal to college students since it is derived from their digital conversations. This type of instructional paradigm shift suggests greater student participation thus increasing the overall sense of an inclusive learning community.

CONCLUSIONS

There is a great debate on what constitutes effective practices in college teaching. However, one component most researchers can agree on is to meet the needs of all students. (Dewey, 1917; Greene, 1978; Marzano, 2003; Noddings, 2006). Today's college students, both traditional and non-traditional, can benefit from the use of inclusive virtual learning communities in their classrooms. This practice can be fun, keep the interest of the college instructor and students, and build upon the notion that students are integral components of their own meaning making. Jones and Lea (2008) contend that, "Early findings are suggesting that the intermingling of institutional and academic textual requirements and issues of student identity and personal affiliation come together to shape the textual interactions of students and their engagement in digital literacies" (p. 214).

Many students entering higher education come from Generation X and Y (Wood, 2006). As this generational gap between college instructors and students, as well as between student and student widens, inclusive college instructors must recognize new methods of meeting their students' needs. As Wood (2006) and Lund (2007) explain, students from generation X and Y have always had computers. In a society powered by instantaneous information, college students deserve the same level of sophistication in their instruction. These technological advances are only going to expand, and inclusive college instructors must use these effective tools to keep students informed and allow them to communicate with their instructors and peers in meaningful ways prescribed by society.

When creating an inclusive virtual learning community, all of the above tools must be evaluated against the objectives and goals of the inclusive learning community being created. Understanding the purpose of the community, the expectations, and the needs of the individuals will allow instructors to select the tool best suited to accomplish the intended learning. For example, individual reflection can be evaluated with an asynchronous tool, whereas group collaboration may require a synchronous tool. Knowing the advantages of each online tool allows instructors to integrate various tools in order to maximize the students' learning experience.

Creating a virtual online community not only consists of various tools and activities, but integrating instructional platforms as well. One main example of integrating technology as a platform in a course is by turning a traditional course into a Hybrid. Hybrid is a way to utilize a technological component to build knowledge and community, as well as keep the traditional face-to-face class aspect. Regardless, the concept is to use both of these ideas to deliver instruction effectively for all college students. In conclusion, an inclusive virtual learning community is an excellent way to create community and to reach all students in the college classroom. Introducing additional technological resources assists in college students' learning, creates a more inclusive learning environment during the course, and hopefully, results in the producing lifelong learners.

REFERENCES

Anastasiades, P., & Retalis, S. (2001). The educational process in the emerging information society: Conditions for the reversal of the linear model of education and the development of an open type hybrid learning environment. *Proceedings of the ED-MEDIA World Conference on Educational Multimedia, Hypermedia & Telecommunications, Tampere, Finland, 1*, 43–48.

Arbaugh, J., & Duray, R. (2002). Technological and structural characteristics, student learning and satisfaction with web-based courses: An exploratory study of two MBA programs. *Management Learning, 33*, 331–347.

Bandura, A. (1977). *Social learning theory*. New York: General Learning Press.

Berners-Lee, T. (1989). Retrieved from http://www.nndb.com/people/573/000023504/.

Blanchard, K., Covey, S. R. et al. (2008). *P-16 Blueprint for success: Proven strategies for success and survival*. Sevierville, TN: Insight Publishing.

Borsook, T. K. (1997). Hypermeidat: Harbinger of a new instructional paradigm? In Dills, C. & Romiszowski, A. (Eds.), *Instructional development state of the art:*

Paradigms and educational technology (pp. 721–744). Englewood Cliffs, NJ: Educational Technology Publications.

Brescia, W., & Miller, M. (2005). Enhancing graduate student performance as threaded discussion leaders in a web-based proposal writing course. *Quarterly Review of Distance Education, 4*(6), 385–396.

Candler, C., Tucker, P., Triplett, J., & Trautman, R. (2006). Using a filter to improve the chatroom experience in interactive medical education. *Medical Teacher, 28*(7), 659–661.

Dewey, J. (1917). *Creative intelligence.* New York: Holt and Company.

Eide, F. (2005). Retrieved from http://eideneurolearningblog.blogspot.com/2005/03/brain-of-blogger.html.

Facebook. (2009). [social network service]. Palo Alto, CA: Facebook Inc. facebook.com

Foster, A. (2007). Professor avatar. The chronicle of higher education. Retrieved from http://chronicle.com/article/Professor-Avatar/30018.

Garnham, C, & Kaleta, R. (2002) Introduction to hybrid courses. Teaching with technology today. University of Wisconsin-Milwaukee. Retrieved from http://www.uwsa.edu/ttt/articles/garnham.htm.

Glasser, W. (1993). *The quality school teacher.* New York: Harper-Collins Publishing.

Graham, C. R., Allen, S., & Ure, D. (2003). *Blended learning environments: A review of the research literature.* Unpublished manuscript, Provo, UT.

Greene, M. (1978). *Landscapes of learning.* New York: Teacher's College Press.

Huffaker, D. (2004, June). The educated blogger: Using weblogs to promote literacy in the classroom. *First Monday, 9*(6). Retrieved from http://firstmonday.org/issues/issue9_6/huffaker/index.

Jones, S., & Lea, M. R. (2008). Digital literacies in the lives of undergraduate students: Exploring personal and curricular spheres of practice. The Electronic Journal of e-Learning, 6(3), 207–216. Available online at www.ejel.org.

Kajder, S., & Bull, G. (2003). Scaffolding for struggling students reading and writing with blogs. *Learning & Leading with Technology, 31*(2), 32–35.

Kittleson, M. J. (2002). Chat room protocol. *American Journal of Health Behavior, 26*(3), 229–230.

Knobel, M., & Lankshear, C. (2004, December). *From pencilvania to pixelandia: Mapping the terrain of new literacies research.* Plenary address presented at the annual National Reading Conference, San Antonio, TX.

Lave, J., & Wenger E. (1991). Situated *learning: Legitimate peripheral participation.* Cambridge: Cambridge University Press.

Leu, D. J., Jr. (2001). Internet project: Preparing students for new literacies in a global village. *The Reading Teacher, 54*(6), 568–572.

Lund, D. (2007). *Digital city: Stepping out and moving through its cyber streets.* Paper presented at the National Reading Conference, Austin, Texas.

MacManus, R. (2006). Social networks gaining on the internet portal. Retrieved from http://www.readwriteweb.com/archives/social_networks_vs_portals.php#

Marzano, R., (2003). *What works in schools.* Alexandria, VA: Association for Supervision & Curriculum.

Maxis Sim-Series. Retrieved from www.underground-gamer.com/.

Minnesota Educational Computing Consortium, MECC (1974). Historical development of Minnesota's instructional computing network. Association for Computing Machinery. *Proceedings of the 1975 annual conference.* New York.

My Space (2009) [social network service]. Beverly Hills, CA: Fox Interactive Media. www.myspace.com

Noddings, N. (2006). *Philosophy of education* (2nd ed.). New York: Westview Press.

Reinking, D., & Bridwell-Bowles, L. (1991). Computers in reading and writing. In R. Barr, M.L. Kamil, P.B. Mosenthal, & P.D. Pearson (Eds.), Handbook of reading research (vol. 2, pp. 310–340). New York: Longman.

Richardson, W. (2006). *Blogs, Wikis, Podcasts, and other powerful web tools for classrooms.* Thousand Oaks: Corwin Press.

Rochman, B. (2009). Twittering in church. Why some pastors are turning to microblogging to bring congregants closer to God and one another. *Time, 173*(21), 51–52.

Ronen, M & Eliahu, M. (1999). Simulation as a home learning environment—Students' views. *Journal of Computer Assisted Learning, 15,* 258–268.

Rowh, M. (2007). E-learning: The anytime, anywhere option. *Career World, 36*(2), 22–25.

Rushkoff, D. (2004). Retrieved from http://rushkoff.com/2005/11/12/get-back-in-the-box-thought-virus-2-open-source-and-the-authorship-society/.

Schallert, D. L., Reed, J. H., & the D-Team. (2003–2004). Intellectual, motivational, textual, and cultural considerations in teaching and learning with computer-mediated discussion. *Journal of Research on Technology in Education, 36,* 103–118.

Second Life Lab. (2003). Retrieved from http://work.secondlife.com/en-US/about/.

Sotillo, S. (2003). Using instant messaging for collaborative learning: A case study. Retrieved from http://www.innovateonline.info/index.php?view=article&id=170.

Vygotsky, L. (1978). Interaction between learning and development. In *Mind in society.* (M. Cole, Trans.). Cambridge, MA: Harvard University Press.

Wang, L., Ertmer, P.A., & Newby, T.J. (2004). Increasing preservice teachers' self-efficacy beliefs for technology integration. *Journal of Research on Technology in Education, 36*(3), 231–252.

Wiki (2009). [website allowing creating and editing of interlinked web pages]. MediaWiki version 1.16alpha-wmf(r59476).

Wood, G. (2006). Recognizing the generational divide: When X meets Y at the tribal college. *Tribal College Journal, 17*(4), 24–25.

YouTube (2009) [video sharing website]. San Bruno, CA: Google Inc. www.youtube.com

CHAPTER 9

THE TECHNOLOGICAL AGE OF TEACHING

Michelle Pulaski Behling and Beth Gordon Klingner

KEY TERMS

Blended Learning; Course Management Systems; Eportfolios; Information
Literacy; Social Networking; Technological Accountability; Web 2.0 Tools

REFLECTIVE QUESTIONS

- Given the latest Web 2.0 tools available, which tools could be readily
  incorporated into the classroom and what will this technology allow
  students to do or achieve?
- What types of projects could instructors incorporate in their courses
  to blend new technologies with traditional face-to- face learning?
- How might instructors teach students to be critical evaluators of the
  information they find online?

Teaching Inclusively in Higher Education, pages 155–169
Copyright © 2010 by Information Age Publishing
All rights of reproduction in any form reserved.

INTRODUCTION

This chapter will discuss the role of instructors in helping students become critical thinkers and competent users of many forms of media. Given today's technological climate, it is essential for students to be savvy in terms of new media. Within their chosen disciplines, students will need to be able to access, manage, and disseminate information via technology. Students come to college with many computer and technological skills, but might not have the ability to apply these skills for deeper thinking and learning in their chosen disciplines. Through the use of Web 2.0 tools such as online social networking, YouTube, course management systems, and eportfolios, students and their instructors can balance the professional standards, accreditation requirements, and mandated learning environments of many programs. Instructors need to carefully select among Web 2.0 tools and match to course content appropriately. It is assumed instructors will take various student learning styles into account as noted in previous chapters. Other factors to consider are course learning objectives, technological hardware and software requirements, and the diverse members of the audience.

When incorporating technology into the teaching and learning experience, instructors can make use of the blended learning approach. *Blended learning* combines traditional face-to-face teaching styles with any number of online instructional methods including course management software and social networking. Blended learning effectively engages students in the learning process by providing them with highly interactive learning experiences that result in the resolution of an issue or problem (Garrison & Vaughan, 2008). In an effort to tap into the online skill set students already possess, instructors can use blended learning techniques to encourage active participation and deeper learning in the classroom.

The blended learning approach offers the advantage of flexibility, convenience, and increased opportunities for interaction with the instructor and other students. Instructors should be well-versed with Web 2.0 tools in order to be able to facilitate students' use of these tools in the discipline or profession. Instructors should be keeping up with emerging technologies as applied to their fields as part of their own continuing instructor development. Blended learning allows students to use tools they are already familiar with to optimize the learning process.

USING TECHNOLOGY TO COMMUNICATE

Today's students, often considered digital natives, are using technology to communicate, socialize, and access information. As illustrated so powerfully by Professor Michael Wesch's (2009) popular YouTube video, *A Vision of Students Today,* there is a strong disconnect between how students are reading and communicating outside of the classroom and how they are being asked to learn within a classroom. Digital natives are defined as those who "have been immersed in technology all of their lives, imbuing them with sophisticated technical skills and learning preferences for which traditional education is unprepared" (Bennett, Maton, & Kervin, 2008, p. 775; refer to Ch. 7 for previous discussion). Many instructors are digital immigrants, having grown up before technology was ubiquitous, and are often reluctant to incorporate emerging technologies into instruction even though today's students read far more websites than books and may prefer online to face time.

The separation of time and space in the online learning setting forces students to be more self-directed and reflective and may even enhance their overall learning. The very nature of higher education must continue to evolve to a more blended format to stay relevant to today's students. Instructors must prepare them for a world in which the technology will continue to change rapidly and the job market will also continue to evolve— forcing students to prepare for a world in which lifelong learning will be essential for job security. It is the instructor's role to help students harness the technological tools that they may already know to their specific profession or workplace. Inclusive instructors will combine their expertise in the field with the appropriate applied technologies.

Instructors must understand that the integration of technology into instruction is not merely for the sake of technology, but for the following essential reasons. The use of technology in the classroom serves to engage and motivate students. Incorporating technological tools into instruction develops information literacy. Critical thinking and learning skills are also enhanced with the integration of technology. In addition, writing and overall communication skills can be greatly improved with the inclusion of technology in the learning process.

Today's instructors may feel that their own digital immigrant status makes it difficult or almost impossible to keep up with the changing technologies or embed technology tools into coursework, but the key point for instructors to realize is that even if students' technological expertise exceeds their own, students still need guidance on how to apply the technologies to the disciplines, how to think critically about the vast amount of information available and how to make effective decisions about the technological tools available. In other words, students need help with *information literacy.* The instructor's role is to create the online environment in which students learn information literacy using technological tools. Further, inclusive instructors must teach their students to critically evaluate what they see online in order to develop into competent media consumers. Information literacy skills will assist them far beyond the time frame of a particular course or semester. Being information literate in today's world is essential for success both professionally and personally.

While students may have the technology skills, they do need help understanding how to access and manage and critique all of the information and technology available. The most effective instructors find ways to incorporate students' tech-savvy abilities into exciting learning opportunities within their disciplines. For example, instructors can encourage students to move beyond Facebooking to creating eportfolios to show off their academic accomplishments. Instructors can help students do more than just "Googling" by showing them how to conduct effective searches through online databases and peer reviewed journals, many now available in fulltext online. Inclusive instructors can help students move beyond texting to twittering about what they are engaged in to show just-in-time learning.

MANAGING THE COURSE WITH TECHNOLOGY

Course management systems are organized tools used to support teaching and learning. Course management systems are essential to developing inclusive learning communities in the virtual world where everyone has an equal opportunity to participate. In a traditional two-hour face-to-face course, discussion is limited by time and may be dominated by a few outspoken individuals, whereas in an online discussion in a course management discussion board, students have ample time to reflect, share and comment. Examples of popular course management systems include Blackboard, Angel, Moodle, and Desire2Learn (refer to Ch. 8 for previous discussion). Initially, course management tools enabled instructors to create web-based course materials without requiring knowledge of HTML or other programming. Often times, the choice of course management systems is made by the university rather than by the individual instructor; however, the instructor typically has control over how best to utilize the system. Many universities rely on course management tools to deliver full online courses and programs and to supplement face-to-face courses.

Web 2.0 Tools

While course management tools have been at the forefront of incorporating technology into instructions, they are quickly falling behind in terms of some of the exciting Web 2.0 tools that are available, often free, through cloud computing. While Web 1.0 tools such as static web pages and the *Encyclopedia Britannica* initially provided great resources for research and knowledge gathering, more interactive *Web 2.0 tools* such as blogs and Wikipedia provide opportunities for participation and collaboration in what Richardson (2009) calls the Read/Write web. Web 2.0 is widely considered the collaborative, social web that exists today. Users actively engage in not only accessing but also creating and commenting on web content. Rather than being merely an encyclopedia of information, Web 2.0 can be a truly interactive learning experience that complements the teaching and learning in and out of the classroom. Tim O'Reilly is credited with coining the term "Web 2.0" at a conference in 2004, but the technology was not really new (Wilen-Daugenti, 2009). What was new was the way it was being used— to create dynamic interfaces containing user-generated content. With Web 2.0 tools, students can consume and create information in multiple ways. The possibilities for teaching and learning with Web 2.0 are vast as inclusive college instructors seek to move beyond delivering content to actually engaging students with the content.

Instructors can use Web 2.0 tools deleting "blogs and wikis" and adding "Web 2.0 tools" instead to engage students in critical thinking and writing in new ways. Whereas Web 1.0 focused on static webpages, Web 2.0 tools allow for easily-created blogs and wikis that do not require any programming expertise to manage. Wikipedia captures the essence of Web 2.0 by gathering information from the wisdom of crowds rather than the traditional panel of a few experts. Richardson (2009) notes "Wikipedia is one of the most important sites for educators to understand. It represents the potential of collaboration on the Web" (p. 56). While many educators object to using Wikipedia as a credible source for information, instructors should keep an open mind about the concept of wikis. Even Wikipedia can be integrated into a lesson on a particular topic. Inclusive instructors will effectively incorporate a variety of teaching tools that positively impact students. Inclusive instructors need to use creativity and sound pedagogical strategies when incorporating emerging technologies. Some examples of ways to embed wikis into curriculum are:

- Have students look up a term or concept on Wikipedia and rewrite the definition to make it more current and relevant.
- Create a course-based wiki to share group projects.
- Create a community wiki to share co-curricular interests with a particular group of students, instructors and alumni.

There are many free wiki tools available such as http://www.wikispaces.com, http://www.wetpaint.com/wiki, and http://pbworks.com. Due to the dynamic nature of Web 2.0 tools, this list may change, but the ideas behind the wiki such as collaboration and participation will probably remain the same. Instructors also need to realize that creating a course-based wiki may pose some philosophical challenges in terms of authorship and intellectual property since wiki collaborators typically have the ability to alter others' writing. The ways in which scholarly writing and plagiarism are viewed will need to be addressed before incorporating a wiki into a course.

RSS Aggregators and Social Bookmarking are Web 2.0 tools that help to organize the flow of information. Many people feel overwhelmed by the amount of information available online. RSS feeds and social bookmarking are two great ways to help educators and students keep current and find meaningful information on topics within their fields. RSS means Real Simple Syndication. This Commoncraft video explains what RSS does in basic terms: http://www.youtube.com/watch?v=0klgLsSxGsU. Essentially, RSS feeds allow users to subscribe to webpages and blogs so that the news that users regularly like to check comes directly to them through a reader. There are many different readers available such as Google, Yahoo, and Outlook. Once a user has established an RSS reader and subscribed to some webpages and blogs, the news comes directly to the user—creating "The Daily Me" (Richardson, 2009, p. 72).

Social Bookmarking is a way of sharing links of common interests. According to Richardson (2009):

> Millions of people have begun using public, online bookmarking services where they can save links, annotate them with unique keywords or "tags" to organize them, and then share them with the world. . . . So social bookmarking sites complete the circle; RSS feeds lets us read and connect with what others write; now we can read and connect with what others read as well. (pp. 88–89)

Sites such as Del.icio.us and Digg help users to see what others are reading and tagging. "RSS lets us read and connect with what others write; now we can read and connect with what others read as well" (Richardson, 2009, p. 89). Both RSS Aggregators and Social Bookmarking tools can be used in a variety of innovative ways by college instructors such as:

- Require students to set up RSS feeds on key topics within a discipline.
- Ask students to share the most interesting online discoveries with others through Del.icio.us and search for other related materials using tags.
- Have students follow a political or local issue through RSS feeds.

Flickr and YouTube are free online image and video sharing services that have revolutionized the way content is shared. Flickr (http://www.flickr.com) encourages users to "share your photos" and "watch the world." What makes this site more than just an online photo album is the tagging, annotating and commenting that occurs, making this truly social software. Tagging is the process of individual's labeling and classifying content on the web. It allows for others to search for items of similar interest and it has been one of the key elements of interactivity and participation of Web 2.0. The annotation feature allows people to label or mark up photos and visitors can add their comments as well. Richardson (2009) notes, "The real power of Flickr lies in the ways it can connect people from around the world" (p. 103). Another interesting element in Flickr is the ability to identify locations of photo, and short videos, via Google's online maps. Through this feature, photos can become part of a larger story that is tracked by location. The power of Flickr is that it allows for students to link to communities outside of the traditional classroom setting. For example, photography students could post their work to Flickr with appropriate tagging and benefit from those tags and comments from other users over time. Flickr is also a fascinating way to follow current events, especially during recent tragedies like Hurricane Katrina where photos were posted to the site instantaneously. Inclusive instructors can utilize this tool to tie their course content to the world at large.

Since 2005, YouTube has encouraged users to "Broadcast Yourself" at http://www.youtube.com. Now owned by Google, when news breaks, it often breaks first on YouTube and then spreads to more traditional sources such as newspapers and television stations. It is easy to upload a video from one's computer or digital camera and then as with Flickr, tagging and commenting become part of the interactive storytelling. Instructors can incorporate YouTube into instruction in a variety of ways. In the same ways that YouTube has been influential in sharing news and entertainment, it can also share exceptional university teaching and thinking. Instructors such as Michael Wesch and Marian Diamond have become university celebrities via YouTube (Wilen-Daugenti, 2009). These instructors have been able to harness the viral nature of the Web and use it to share their expertise. Inclusive instructors can learn from their success by also creating mini-lectures on YouTube to reach a global audience.

Instructors can use Flickr and YouTube and other file-sharing services to help create and share stories within their own disciplines. Alexander and Levine (2008) write about Web 2.0 storytelling as the emergence of a new genre. Social Media allows for "stories that open-ended, branching, hyperlinked, cross-media, participatory, exploratory, and unpredictable" (Alexander & Levine, 2008, p. 40). Some ways in which Flickr and YouTube can be integrated into instruction are:

- Show film clips with a history or English class.
- Include YouTube clips of famous speeches in a speech course.
- Show pictures/videos of natural disasters in an environmental studies course.
- Show current events pictures/videos to spark a discussion in any discipline.

- Use the mapping feature in Flickr to take a virtual field trip.
- Assign students a presentation that incorporates either video or photo sharing elements.

Social Networking including tools such as Facebook http://www.facebook.com, LinkedIn http://www.linkedin.com, and Twitter http://twitter.com are gaining in popularity in mainstream culture, yet still remain somewhat outside of the classroom experience. Instructors who are able to incorporate social networking tools will find that they can engage, motivate, and even enhance the learning experience for today's digital native students. For many instructors, this process remains daunting since the tools are changing so rapidly. By the time of publication of this text, there will probably be other tools to add to the list. Also, some instructors are skeptical about the academic applications of these tools since so much is written about these tools being used in social settings. But in a process of consumerization, many of these tools can be explored in a personal setting at first and then later applied to an academic setting.

Facebook, LinkedIn, and Twitter are ways in which people can connect with one another based on similar interests and networks. Facebook started as a way for college students to connect with one another, but has expanded tremendously. LinkedIn is more of a professional social networking site allowing connections to be made and professional job histories and consulting interests to be shared. Twitter is a micro-blogging service that requires users to share their thoughts in 140 characters or less per tweet. This tool often draws much skepticism because of its limitations in space and its use by many celebrities and non-celebrities to post trivial messages. But Twitter's global impact has often been underestimated as well its academic potential.

College students are already using these tools, so the challenge to instructors is to find ways to engage them in academic purposes. Some possible examples include:

- Create a Facebook Group page for a course and require students to have discussions and share resources through this page.
- Use LinkedIn to connect with Alumni in fields related to current students' interests to arrange internships or shadow programs.
- Use Twitter to send out announcements, reminders or links related to a course topic.

TECHNOLOGICAL ACCOUNTABILITY

With all the technology tools students will be using in the classroom, instructors are often left wondering how they will evaluate their students' use of these skills. Initially, instructors need to be accountable for knowing, selecting, and using technology effectively. At the same time, students must learn and also be held *accountable for the technology* and how it applies to a given discipline. Inclusive instructors may take the following into consideration when evaluating student work:

1. Use rubrics to guide and assess student work.
2. Implement formative and summative assessment.
3. Employ Chickering and Gamson's (1991) Seven Principles of Good Practice.
4. Require students to create eportfolios to showcase their work.

Rubrics are scoring tools used to evaluate a given piece of work based on a set of criteria (Andrade, 2000; refer to Ch. 7 for discussion). Rubrics set clear guidelines for students so they can meet instructor expectations and course requirements. For example, if instructors require students to participate in online course discussions, a rubric for the discussion posts would include specifics on the quality and quantity of the responses as well as deadlines.

Rubrics can also help students become better judges of their own work and the work of others (Andrade, 2000). Through repeated use of rubrics in self and peer assessment, students are better able to identify and solve problems in their work. Rubrics are easy to use and can save instructors time in the grading process. Instead of writing a detailed explanation for a grade in an online course, instructors can just refer students to the posted rubric. The use of rubrics often results in better student learning and improved work quality. Students are better able to articulate what they have learned when rubrics are used. The use of rubrics assists in the development of the competent media consumer by showing exactly what is expected and how each project will be evaluated. Rubrics prepare students for professional roles by highlighting criteria for performance. Through the use of rubrics students can begin to anticipate how their work will be viewed by others both in the classroom and the professional world.

Both formative and summative assessments should be used to evaluate student use of Web 2.0 tools. Formative assessments are part of the instructional process and aid instructors in adjusting their teaching during the learning progression. An example of formative assessment would be giving students verbal feedback on their blogs versus assigning them grades. Encouraging peers to comment on a student's photography project posted on Flickr would be another way in which formative assessment can be used to evaluate students' Web 2.0 skills.

Summative assessments are typically used to assign a grade to a given project or course. These assessments are usually given at the end of a learning period to evaluate the effectiveness of student performance. Examples of summative assessments include tests, projects, and papers. Instructors may use summative assessments to evaluate various Web 2.0 skills from the efficacy of Wikipedia entries to the popularity of a student-created poetry blog.

The Seven Principles of Good Practice (Chickering & Gamson, 1987) were originally designed to help instructors examine individual student behaviors and improve teaching and learning in the traditional face to face classroom. However, the principles can also be used to evaluate learning in the online environment. The seven principles include:

1. Faculty-student contact;
2. Cooperation among students;
3. Active learning;
4. Prompt feedback;
5. Emphasizing time on task;
6. Communicating high expectations; and
7. Respecting diverse talents and ways of learning.

The first principle (faculty-student contact) highlights instructors' involvement and availability to students. In the online classroom, instructors need to set clear guidelines for student email requests. Students should provide a clear subject line and identify the course they are taking in the subject line or email body. Instructors must clearly outline the response time for student emails so students realize that a reply is not always immediate.

Chickering and Gamson's (1987) second principle of cooperation among students gets a boost with Web 2.0 tools. Today students can join social networking groups to connect with others. Students can now evaluate their peers' work online using the file-sharing features of course management systems. Online discussion boards can also be set up to assist meaningful cooperation among students.

Student presentations can be included in online courses to encourage active learning, which is the third principle. Posting PowerPoint presentations or case studies to a course site allows for student feedback and students can make changes to their presentations based on their peers' responses (Graham et al., 2001). Not only is this skill helpful in the classroom, but it can also be applied to professional disciplines and team problem solving.

The fourth principle, prompt feedback, can be incorporated in the classroom in the form of online quizzes and tests. Online technology also provides instructors with a means to contact students more frequently than face to face interaction allows. Online survey tools will also allow for immediate in class feedback for both instructor and students. Graham et al. (2001) suggest instructors give two types of feedback: "information feedback" and "acknowledgment feedback." Information feedback is given when instructors answer a quick email question while acknowledgement feedback occurs when confirmation is sent that an assignment is received (Graham et al., 2001).

Students need to adhere to deadlines according to Chickering and Gamson's (1987) fifth principle, emphasizing time on task. Setting up clear deadlines in an online course allows students to know instructor expectations and aides them in organizing their time online. Online course management systems can be used to post homework assignments so students can easily hand in assignments on time if they are absent.

In terms of communicating high expectations, the sixth principle, instructors can post examples of past student work online for current classes to model (Graham et al., 2001). In online discussion boards, instructors can easily highlight strong posts for other students to follow. Instructors should email or post course progress to keep students on track. Referring students to course rubrics is also suggested.

In order to foster a respect for diverse talents and ways of learning, the seventh principle, students should adhere to proper netiquette. Netiquette involves the respectful and courteous exchange of ideas in an online environment. Netiquette rules or guidelines can be set for each course to ensure politeness and avoid harassment (Holeton, 1988). The netiquette policy should be included in the syllabus or prominently featured in an online course. The following is an example of a netiquette policy and may be used in online courses:

> Netiquette is defined as "Using technology to effectively communicate with others both personally and professionally with knowledge, understanding, and courtesy" (http://www.netmanners.com/). Online exchanges can be difficult to interpret because we can't hear a person's tone or see a person's body language. Because of these limitations, it is especially important for each of us to think carefully about what we "say" online. Ask yourselves, "Would I say this to someone's face?" Remember to show your peers, and me, the same respect you wish to be shown.

Eportfolios are digital collections of student work created over a given period of time. Eportfolios showcase students' understanding of concepts and skills while providing an opportunity for self-reflection. Web 2.0 tools can easily be incorporated in the eportfolio process. For example, students can create YouTube videos of their speeches and post them to their eportfolios for peers to comment on. Wikis can also be used to create opportunities for student interaction and feedback. The eportfolio then becomes a type of digital résumé for students when it can be shared with a public audience. Figure 9.1 shows how to integrate Web 2.0 tools with practical assignments in a range of disciplines. This will aid instructors in effectively incorporating technology in their courses.

Practical Considerations (Best Practices)

Web 2.0 Tool	Sample Assignment
Wikis	Create a course-based wiki to share group projects in a business course.
RSS feeds	Have students follow a health issue through RSS feeds.
Social Bookmarking	Ask students to share political current events with others through Digg.
Flickr	Use the mapping feature in Flickr to take a virtual field trip for a history course.
YouTube	Include YouTube clips of famous speeches in a Speech course.
Facebook	Create a Facebook Group page for a course.
LinkedIn	Use LinkedIn to connect with Alumni to arrange internships.
Twitter	Use twitter to send out announcements, or links related to a course topic.

FIGURE 9.1.   Web 2.0 Best Practices.

Rubric

Assignment: Create a blog related to course materials. Include course concepts in the blog content. Posts to the blog must be made at least once a week. Students must also post on classmates' blogs.

Instructions

Create a blog related to course materials. Include course concepts in the blog content. Posts to the blog must be made at least once a week. Students must also post on classmates' blogs.

3: Excellent

2: Good

1: Satisfactory

0: Unsatisfactory

Course Blog				
Timeliness: Met all assigned deadlines	0	1	2	3
Communication: Expressed thoughts clearly	0	1	2	3
Writing: Proper spelling, grammar, punctuation	0	1	2	3
Initiative/Motivation: Made suggestions on other student work and implemented feedback	0	1	2	3
Application to discipline: Incorporated class concepts	0	1	2	3
Real World Application: Related project to current events	0	1	2	3
Creativity: Included unusual viewpoints and ideas	0	1	2	3
Appearance: Project visuals appropriate and easy to follow	0	1	2	3

FIGURE 9.2.   Customizable Web 2.0 Rubric.

A simple rubric designed by both students and teachers should be created for evaluating eportfolios. Components such as graphic elements, active hyperlinks, personal reflections, and the development of peer reflection can be evaluated in the eportfolio rubric. Instructors are also advised to incorporate rubrics when evaluating student use of Web 2.0 tools. Figure 9.2 contains a general rubric for blog assignments. The rubric can be adjusted by discipline and assignment.

CONCLUSIONS

Inclusive college instructors are facing many challenges in the classroom today. Students are texting, instant messaging, twittering, and exploring the latest social networking tools available. One possible way of engaging today's college students is to incorporate some of these tools in such as way that they add to the learning experience and help to create competent media consumers. Instructors should help students develop their online social networking skills into more professional forms such as eportfolios. Moving beyond posting photographs and friending, instructors can teach students the benefits of publishing strong academic accomplishments in eportfolios and networking through LinkedIn. The goal is to create information literate students within a discipline who will continue to be lifelong learners and remain competent media consumers. Using a blended learning approach, inclusive instructors can incorporate course management systems

TABLE 9.1. Instructor Resources

1. Chickering, A., & Gamson, Z. (1987). Seven principles of good practice in undergraduate education. *AAHE Bulletin, 39,* 3–7.

   The authors describe seven key principles designed to help instructors examine individual student behaviors and improve teaching and learning in the classroom.

2. www.epsilen.com

   The software system provides eportfolio and social networking services to users. Epsilen offers a repository for the creation and storage of learning objects in electronic format.

3. Multimedia Educational Resource for Learning and Online Teaching: http://www.merlot.org/

   The online community comprised of faculty, staff, and students from around the world provides peer reviewed teaching and learning materials along with pedagogical strategies.

4. Tomorrow's Professor Listserv Stamford University: http://ctl.stanford.edu/Tomprof/index.shtml

   The fully moderated list seeks to foster a diverse, world-wide teaching and learning ecology among its subscribers. The list contains hundreds of archived posts.

and Web 2.0 tools to motivate students and enhance learning by adapting the selected technologies to match learning styles (See Table 9.1 for additional resources).

Although more research needs to be done in this area to determine the best ways to incorporate emerging technologies and to assess what improvements are made, it is clear that both instructors and students need to be technologically accountable. Instructors demonstrate technology responsibility by staying current with emerging technologies and by introducing their applications to students within their discipline. Students demonstrate technology responsibility by learning the appropriate ways to use the tools both for their learning and for their careers.

REFERENCES

Alexander, B., & Levine, A. (2008, Nov–Dec). Web 2.0 storytelling: Emergence of a new genre. *EDUCAUSE Review, 43*(6), pp. 40, 42, 44, 46–48, 50–52, 54, 56.

Andrade, H. G. (2000). Using rubrics to promote thinking and learning. *Educational Leadership, 57*(5), 13–18.

Angel. (2009). [course management software program]. Washington, DC: Blackboard Inc. www.blackboard.com

Bennett, S., Maton, K., & Kervin, L. (2008). The 'digital natives' debate: A critical review of the evidence. *British Journal of Educational Technology, 39*(5), 775–786.

Blackboard (2009) [educational software]. Washington, DC: Backboard Inc. www.blackboard.com

Chickering, A., & Gamson, Z. (1987). Seven principles of good practice in undergraduate education. *AAHE Bulletin, 39*, 3–7.

Del.icio.us. (2009). [online social bookmarking]. Sunnyvale, CA: Yahoo! Inc. http://delicious.com

Desire2Learn. (2009). [educational software]. Kitchener, Ontario, Canada: Desire2Learn. www.desire2learn.com

Digg. (2009). [social news service]. San Francisco: Digg. www.digg.com

Facebook. (2009). [social network service]. Palo Alto, CA: Facebook Inc. facebook.com

Flickr. (2009). [image and video hosting website]. Sunnyvale, CA: Yahoo! Inc. Flickr.com

Garrison, D. R., & Vaughan, N. D. (2008). *Blended learning in higher education.* San Francisco, CA: Jossey-Bass.

Graham, C., Cagiltay, K., Lim, B., Craner, J., & Duffy, T. M. (2001). Seven principles of effective teaching: A practical lens for evaluating online courses. The Technology Source. Retrieved July 13, 2009 from The Technology Source: http://technologysource.org/article/seven_principles_of_effective_teaching/

Holeton, R. (1988). *Composing cyberspace identity, community, and knowledge in the electronic age.* McGraw Hill: Boston.

LinkedIn. (2009). [professional network service]. Mountain View, CA: LinkedIn. www.inkedin.com

Moodle. (2009). [course management software program]. Perth, Australia: Moodle. www.moodle.org

Netmanners.com: Using Technology with Knowledge, Understanding and Courtesy (http://www.netmanners.com/).

Richardson, W. (2009). *Blogs, wikis, podcasts, and other powerful web tools for classrooms.* Thousand Oaks, CA: Corwin Press.

RRS. (2009). [web application/rss+xml]. Indiana University-Purdue University, Indianapolis

Twitter. (2009). [social network service, micro-blogging]. San Francisco, CA: Twitter. www.twitter.com

Wesch, M. (2009). [YouTube video]. *A vision of students today* retrieved from http://www.youtube.com/watch?v=dGCJ46vyR9o

Wiki. (2009). [website allowing creating and editing of interlinked web pages]. MediaWiki version 1.16alpha-wmf(r59476).

Wilen-Daugenti, T. (2009). *edu: Technology and learning environments in higher education.* Peter Lang Publishing.

YouTube. (2009). [video sharing website]. San Bruno, CA: Google Inc. www.youtube.com

CHAPTER 10

APPLICATIONS TO INCLUSIVE COLLEGE CLASSROOMS

Moira A. Fallon, Susan C. Brown, and Alexander B. Casareno

The following scenarios have been developed based on real college class-rooms and the efforts of real inclusive college instructors. They are provided for the purpose of demonstrating the application of the various instructional techniques described in this text. In reviewing these scenarios, the authors suggest that readers ask themselves the following:

1. Is the scenario described similar to any situation that I have been in while teaching in higher education?
2. What aspects of the scenario can I take back to my own discipline and content?
3. What adjustments to my courses would I have to make in order to implement the techniques described?

APPLICATION SCENARIO #1: INTRODUCTION TO PSYCHOLOGY COURSE AT THE LOCAL COMMUNITY COLLEGE

Overview of Scenario #1

Dr. Jeffers looked over the class list for his Introduction to Psychology class. This was his second year of teaching at Green Acres Community Col-

Teaching Inclusively in Higher Education, pages 171–184
Copyright © 2010 by Information Age Publishing
All rights of reproduction in any form reserved.

lege. This semester's class had 73 students in it, approximately 54% were female and 46% were males. He sighed just a little. So many of his students do not want to take the class, but are required to by their programs. This meant to him that they were reluctant students.

He also immediately notices that his class is very diverse in terms of the potential majors of his students and the number of credit hours already taken. Another sigh escapes. The students who have taken more hours generally have a better approach to the academic workload in his course. He decides to delve a little deeper into the class list. "Perhaps I can improve my course if I make some adjustments to my teaching," he thinks aloud. He has generally used a lecture format the two times he has previously taught the course. Lecture seems to fit the course content and the large numbers of students who have to take the class.

Dr. Jeffers sent out an automatic message when students registered for his class. Not all of the community college instructors choose to do this. However, he feels it can really benefit him with his course planning. He has put the responses into a spreadsheet and compiled the following information from his course-management system. The information compiled is based on the registration information each student supplied.

Individual needs matrix for class: Based on the students' responses to his automatic message, Dr. Jeffers now has the following information about this group of students:

- 73 students registered for this class.
- 39 are female and 34 are male.
- 56 students are typical ages of 18–25 years old, while 17 are 35+ years old.
- 69 students speak English as first language, while four students speak Spanish.
- 15% of the students attended a more affluent suburban high school, while the remainder attended public high schools in the city central part of town.
- Most of the students are from lower-middle class families, which is also reflected in the community at large.
- Four students are members of migrant families who work at the local farms.
- 80% of students are Caucasian, with 20% of minority ethnicities.
- Three students have a learning disability. One student has a history of depression.
- More than half of the students have not determined a major and are taking the class to fulfill one of their general education credits. Ten students intend to become teachers, five students plan to be nurses,

one wants to be a scientist, three plan on English literature, and two want to be meteorologists.

Given this information, Dr. Jeffers decides to make some initial adjustments to his class in hopes of improving his teaching and including all of his students. This is difficult due to the large numbers of students and the lecture format of the class. However, after pondering for some time, he decides upon the following adjustments to his class:

Course Adjustments for Scenario #1

Dr. Jeffers reviews a number of potential course adjustments, weighing them for appropriateness to his students and to the course content. He reviews his plan with Dr. Prince, the CELT administrator. Together, they come up with the following plan for his course:

1.   Dr. Jeffers decides to use Power Point slides for his lectures. He has added pictures and videos plus mixed media. They will also contain written content information, visual pictures, group discussion topics, and practice questions.
2.   He will add advanced organizers each day. They will be posted on the first slide of his Power Points. He will review them orally at the beginning and end of his lecture with the entire class.
3.   He will use the laser pointer Clickers with close-ended, multiple choice questions. He can check the Clickers out from his department without a cost to the students. He can use the Clicker devices to gauge both individual and group performance.
4.   Dr. Jeffers decides that he will have one discussion question assigned to the whole class each week. Students will be randomly placed into small groups and required to orally share with the class their conclusions. The questions for discussion will be focused on examples and impacts of course content. Students will be asked to submit a written one-page summary of their conclusions after the small group discussion has taken place to hand in at the next class period.

Dr. Jeffers thinks these are small changes to make initially, but is eager to see the effects of his changes upon his class. He thinks it would be best to implement some ongoing assessments to determine the effectiveness of these proposed teaching changes.

Ongoing Assessments used to Evaluate Teaching Effectiveness

The decision to monitor the implementation of the course adjustments is a good one. He determines that he will utilize the following assessments which will be administered throughout the course to determine the effects of his proposed course adjustments:

- Pretest of the basic vocabulary and terminology;
- Discussion questions and written conclusions from small group discussion;
- Clicker responses for individuals and large group; and
- Post test on key concepts and vocabulary at the end of the course.

Summary of Scenario #1

Overall, as Dr. Jeffers reflects upon the changes he made to his Introduction to Psychology class, he is pleased with the results. "I am glad that I was able to implement some instructional changes and on the whole I believe they were effective for the students," he thinks. He knows there isn't just one right way to teach this course, but he really wants to continue to improve his teaching. He also wants to review his teaching across time with this same course and with the different groups of students. "This will help me to better improve my scholarship of teaching," he says aloud. He decides to analyze the course's ongoing assessments for this group of students and to compare against the previous students and for the next time he teaches the course. He determines to reflect upon the pre- and post-test results for individual and group performances and for content improvement. So he organizes the information from the pre- and post-testing, along with the results of the Clickers on the practice questions into a spreadsheet. This will help with the comparison across time and groups.

He continues to reflect upon his teaching and the self evaluation he is doing with this course. "My successes in teaching have been directly related to the successes of my students in their learning processes," he determines. However, to really improve his scholarship of teaching he knows he is going to have to seek additional outside experts for more ideas for teaching improvement. "I really want to increase the active learning process of each of my students. That is hard in a class of this size." In particular, he reflects that he would like to improve his application of technology to this introductory class. He plans to attend some conferences that promote the use of technology in the field of psychology. "It is my goal to embed into every course I teach and every program that I plan effective research-based methods and instructional strategies that I model and use with my students," Dr. Jeffers concludes. "It may not be perfect, but I will be satisfied if I keep trying and getting better."

APPLICATION SCENARIO #2: HONORS CLASS IN GENDER AND EDUCATION: CROSS-CULTURAL PERSPECTIVES

Overview of Scenario #2

A college honors class titled *Gender and Education: Cross-Cultural Perspectives* had 35 undergraduate students, 30 women and five men. All students were of traditional college age and in their junior or senior year at the large university. They came from a wide variety of majors, including pre-medical, history, economics, business, and education. There were five international students: two women from India, one woman from Argentina, one man from Russia, and one woman from Taiwan. All students had been selected for this course based on their academic abilities and achievements, so the instructor, Dr. Johnson, knew that she would have to challenge them academically. In addition, she realized that building interpersonal relationships would be very important for creating a safe and secure classroom environment where all students were free to express their opinions.

Dr. Johnson selected one text for the first half of the course, which was focused on American gender issues in education. For the second half, the course readings were to be primarily research articles from studies done in a variety of countries. She arranged to have these articles available online through the university library. In addition, Dr. Johnson arranged to have two copies of the text put on reserve at the library. The course syllabus included the specific topics to be covered each class period, appropriate readings to be done in advance, and reflective questions to be answered in one to two pages. One major component of the course was a group project where each small group of three to four students would choose a country to research the educational system and issues of gender in education.

Course Adjustments for Scenario #2

During the first class period of the semester, Dr. Johnson made several observations about her students. She noted that the two women from India wore the traditional headdress and clothing for Muslims and sat close to each other at one of the six-person round tables in the room. The five men in the class were all sitting together at a table in the back of the room. Few of the students knew each other and most seemed ready for instructor to dispense academic information rather than enjoying the opportunity to get acquainted with other students.

Starting class, Dr. Johnson began by introducing herself and telling the class about her own academic background and interests. She deliberately included enough personal information about her international experiences so that the students could get a sense of who she was and what world view and perspectives she might bring to the course. Next, she gave an overview of the course and the syllabus, talking about major assignments and course expectations and reassuring the students that she would further discuss these as the semester progressed. Then Dr. Johnson had students talk with each other at the tables to learn about each other's majors and interests and to share something unique or unusual about themselves. She explained that students were to introduce the student sitting on their right side. As the individual students introduced each other, she noticed that the man from Russia and the woman from Taiwan had strong accents and were difficult to understand. The Taiwanese woman tended to speak softly and hesitantly, making it very hard for other students to hear her.

After the first class, the instructor thought back about her initial impressions and concerns. She wanted to make sure that the students felt comfortable enough in the class to move away from their chosen positions and classroom companions. She also wanted all students to be able to express their opinions even on difficult issues or discussions and she did not want eager students to dominate the discussions. She decided to use the one-page reflections given in the syllabus as a way for guided student interaction, as well as ongoing assessment of student understanding. Since the reflections were to be written after the readings were done but before class discussion, she planned for paired and small group sharing followed by whole-class reporting. Sometimes she would allow students to pair and then share at their original tables, but other times she would have three students from each six-student table move to another table.

As the students became more comfortable in the class, Dr. Johnson used different ways to arrange new student groupings and individual student roles. Assigning student roles, an important part of cooperative learning, assured that all students had a chance to be group leaders of discussions, recorders of the discussions, observers of the process, and reporters to the whole class. In this way, students who were more quiet or hesitant to speak up were included in small-group and whole-class discussions. Since the reporters were not expressing their own opinion but were relating group comments from the recorders' notes, the international students particularly gained in confidence over the semester.

During the semester, Dr. Johnson incorporated technology into the course by using Power Point for main concepts, videos for national and international documentaries on gender in education issues, and the Internet for websites such as UNESCO and UNICEF. She also arranged a review and preview section based on student comments from the previous class session, which she had originally written on the white board and then copied after class. Because the students were generally comfortable with technology and many of its possibilities, she indicated that their research projects had to have solid research based on reliable Internet sources, a multi-media presentation, and an interactive section applying the main themes of the research findings.

During the semester, Dr. Johnson also used two available human resources to speak to the class. The first was Fulbright Professor Petrov from Moscow, Russia. Dr. Johnson shared her syllabus with him and prepared an information sheet with generic themes and reflective questions from the course. Dr. Johnson also arranged for Dr. Petrov to attend several class sessions to meet the students and interact with them. Together the whole class prepared a series of questions they wanted Dr. Petrov to answer during her speech the next class session. The second resource was the father of the Argentinean woman. She had mentioned early in the semester that her father would be glad to speak to the class. Dr. Johnson made the arrangements through the student, asking her to give her father the syllabus and the questions the students prepared in advance. Both presenters were well received by the class members, who were asked in advance to be ready with additional questions if needed.

Summary on Scenario #2

After the semester had finished, Dr. Johnson reflected on what other kinds of adjustments she could have made to enrich the students' course experiences. One main consideration was the research project. Given the type of students involved and the very specific assignment sheet for the project, the quality of research was not a major problem, but the use of Power Points and time allotment were. The small groups of students had prepared so much information that they had trouble fitting it into their time slot of 60 minutes, so they raced through their Power Points and cut short the class activities and discussions during the required interactive part. Students needed more instruction on how to balance their mini-lecture presentation with class involvement. Some groups needed help with keeping Power Points to a few words and major ideas for each slide. In general, the groups needed more instructor assistance in becoming facilitators of learning rather than dispensers. Students (and she herself) could also learn to use more instructional strategies such as concept mapping and stick figure illustrations done in real time to help their classmates process the main points of their presentation.

One unanticipated outcome with the group projects came from Dr. Johnson's allowing international students to research their own countries' policies and practices in education. The project on India not only had the personal perspectives of the Indian women on their early schooling, but the project freed the women to talk about their religious practices. One of the women related her experience of attending a private Catholic school in India. Most of the international students also admitted that they knew almost nothing about public education in their countries because they were from privileged social classes and had attended only private schools. Dr. Johnson decided to include the project option for international students in the future and to expand the curriculum to include more about class and gender, emphasizing more why girls generally receive less education when families and countries are poor.

The inclusion of the guest speakers added an authentic part to the course, but the student questions were not as organized and thoughtful as they could have been. In addition, having students ask questions that the speakers might not be able to answer was a real risk. Dr. Johnson decided that the next time guest speakers were involved that the class would prepare in advance a list of questions to be asked. Using a KWL chart could aid this process by focusing students on what important concepts need to be covered. The questions about what students want to learn, and what instructors want them to learn, could then be given in advance to the speakers. If guest speakers were invited in the earlier part of the semester, the KWL chart could also guide the students for their own group presentations.

Another good possibility for modifying techniques in the future was the weekly reflective question assignments connected to the readings. Dr. Johnson thought that at least some of these could be done online using blogs. In this way, the students could be sharing their thoughts out of class as well as in class. Using blogs would have the additional advantage of freeing up class time that was needed for guest speakers, international videos on gender issues, and other course content. Dr. Johnson still planned to include some in-class discussions, particularly at the beginning of the semester so that she could give instant feedback on the quality of responses and monitor which students felt comfortable in small- and whole-group discussions.

APPLICATION SCENARIO #3: PRIVATE FOUR YEAR COLLEGE: WELCOME TO CHEMISTRY ONE!

Overview of Scenario #3

In an introductory chemistry course at a prestigious private university on the west coast of the U.S., Lee starts every semester with these words: "Welcome to Chemistry One. In this course we will learn how the discipline of chemistry allows us to live better lives. But only some of you will learn that. By mid-term, one-quarter of you will be gone. By the final, another quarter will either choose to withdraw or will plan on repeating the course if you want the course as a prerequisite for the nursing program or as pre-med or pre-dental program."

Lee has been a chemistry professor for 22 years and in the last seven years, his university has begun to experience a tremendous shift and growth in the student population. Lee is a very good and caring professor who wants students to succeed and to reach their personal and academic goals. But, typically Chemistry One at his university starts as a lecture with 300+ students and while Lee hopes that those 300 freshman will be successful in their college goals, he understands that success in his course necessarily starts with being able to critically read the required textbook so as to make meaning out of the chemistry taught in the book, in the lecture and in the lab section. Lab instructors also have a textbook they use and those instructors and Lee report that while students do read the books, they also tend to not read them that well. The top students memorize terms and formulas and are able to make connections between those terms and formulas and the problems of the lab or the theme of the lectures. The students who struggle tend to memorize terms and formulas, but don't know much beyond that. On short answer tests and lab demonstrations these students can't apply what they have learned and on multiple-choice portions of tests, they do well only on those questions where terms and formulas are explained directly as they were memorized. Lee believes that learning to think critically as scientists requires students to think critically as they read, yet he also believes that he doesn't know how to teach that way.

Course Adjustments for Scenario #3

Lee decided to start with implementation of a course management system. His university recently adopted Blackboard, but Lee had not taken the time previously to learn how the system worked. He started by attending a workshop given by the CELT staff in order to familiarize himself with the properties of Blackboard. As he learned the system, he was delighted to find that it could make his task of redesigning his course easier. He decided to send his Power Points ahead of class to all students. He included with the Power Point slides a listing of the major concepts and vocabulary terms he planned to cover that day. He also included a final slide, briefly summarizing the critical content covered, using a One Sentence Summary (OSS). He planned to have students create their own OSS once he had modeled and they were used to the strategy.

Lee began infusing his lectures with examples of how chemistry may matter to a person pursuing a career in the health sciences. For example, he challenged students to discuss how certain recreational drugs might react together with prescription drugs in a person given the known side effects of the prescription medication and the effects those recreational drugs have had on individuals. Lee noticed that students seemed more interested in his lecture when he provided such examples and wondered if when given meaning, chemistry has more purpose for students other than that it fulfills a requirement for a major.

Along with interactive examples, Lee also felt that the discipline of chemistry was uniquely suited to the use of cartoons and pictures. He decided to have his students draw out their formulas using a software program with mapping and pictorial capabilities. He thought it would be a great idea to have his students post their work on the formulas using Flickr. All students must post their work at least once a semester and every student must respond to a posting (not their own) once a semester. He planned to grade the postings and responses with a rubric designed for that work. As Lee reviewed his plans for adjusting his chemistry course, he realized that most of the strategies he planned on implementing would generate information for him to assess the effectiveness of his teaching and the learning of his students.

Summary of Scenario #3

Lee is very aware that the top students in his lecture will be successful in their chosen majors because they already know how to study and know how to learn by applying the knowledge learned to other situations. Lee also is aware that some, if not many, of the students who struggle and those that leave or fail his course do so because they do not have strong study skills or strong reading skills that will allow them to learn. That so many of these students who struggle are of ethnic minorities also cannot be denied and Lee feels the responsibility to teach in such a way so as to engage those students. Having taken the time to ask these students about their goals and their life histories, which Lee now does at the beginning of every semester, he reports that these students were often at the top of their high school classes and know what they want and why they want it.

If it is the case that students who are bright and motivated and have been admitted to a prestigious university will have difficulty learning, what's an instructor to do? As the populations of colleges and universities become more diverse, a question the inclusive college instructor must ask seems to be: How do we teach so as to reach these new learners? Lee has noticed that motivation and ability exist for his students, and he has learned that when connecting to students' prior knowledge about chemical reactions of recreational drugs and prescription medication, students rise to the occasion and have something to say about the chemistry he is teaching. An interesting footnote to Lee's journey in evolving his instructional strategies for teaching chemistry: The following semester Lee was asked by his chair to redesign his class as a fully online course. Lee objected for a variety of reasons, not the least of which was his desire to continue his efforts to engage his students in an inclusive learning environment. Lee was allowed to continue the chemistry course in a classroom setting. However, he is sure that efforts to put the course online will continue.

APPLICATION SCENARIO #4: GRADUATE SEMINAR IN POLITICAL SCIENCE

Overview of Scenario #4

Dr. Dennison left her chair's office. She had just been told that she was next in line to take her turn to teach the graduate seminar class for the department. All of the faculty members take their turns with the class. It is an elective course for the department's graduate students. The class meets for a three and a half hour block of time each week for the semester. The last time she had taught it was two years ago, when she was fresh out of her doctoral program. She is competent with technology as her doctoral program utilized a variety of technological tools for all the doctoral students. In this sense she is different from some of her current colleagues. At 29 years of age, Dr. Dennison is younger than many of her students. This is not a problem for her in general. She enjoys teaching and enjoys interacting with her students. She loves the idea of creating an interactive classroom community.

Dr. Dennison's college is a public, four-year institution with a rich history in the region of the United States in which it is located. The population of local community is approximately 33,000. There are four other colleges or universities in the area. However, her college is the most affordable for the generally middle and lower class population that makes up the largely blue collar workforce. The city itself has a city center with residential and suburban communities nearby. When Dr. Dennison moved to the area to begin her career in higher education, she noted that her institution frequently had students who are not digital natives. She is very competent in technology and came from schools that had a variety of technology available for faculty and students alike. She has been surprised in the past when not all of her students were able to financially afford technology fees and textbooks.

Some of the students who elected to take the class were beginning to think about their thesis. This semester she had thirteen students registered to take the class. All of the students were matriculated and seeking a Master's degree in Political Science with a subspecialty area. The department's requirements for this course were quite specific. Students were expected to complete a small research project during the course and also to have completed a detailed proposal for a larger study suitable for their thesis. She realized all of her students were taking this course, not from a love of research or statistics, but rather because it was required. Since this was a graduate course, there was a textbook plus a variety of readings, generally averaging 50-60 pages per week.

Student Characteristics

	Student Ages	Gender	Digital Native	ESL	Financial Need	Ethnicity	Disability
1.	33 years	F	No	No	Yes	Caucasian	Yes
2.	26 years	M	Yes	No	Yes	Black	No
3.	27 years	M	Yes	No	Yes	Black	No
4.	41 years	F	No	No	Yes	Black	No
5.	56 years	M	No	No	No	Black	Yes
6.	22 years	F	Yes	Yes	Yes	Asian	No
7.	22 years	F	Yes	Yes	Yes	Hispanic	No
8.	36 years	F	No	No	No	Black	Yes
9.	29 years	M	Yes	No	No	Caucasian	No
10.	25 years	M	Yes	Yes	Yes	Hispanic	No
11.	24 years	F	Yes	No	Yes	Caucasian	No
12.	31 years	M	No	No	No	Caucasian	No
13.	28 years	M	Yes	No	Yes	Caucasian	No

Course Adjustments for Scenario #4

The 13 students in the course were able to receive a great deal of college instructor assistance. The small class size allowed for the formation of a positive in-classroom community. However, Dr. Dennison found from the beginning of the course that her students did not understand or appreciate the importance of either research or statistics to their daily lives. She felt that if she could get her students to strategically read the text they would have a better understanding of research methods. So she introduced the idea of doing partner reads in groups of two with the sharing of textbook. In this way better reading, use of vocabulary, and understanding of concepts could take place. She asked each of the students to develop an individual SQ3R during their buddy reading. She could then use the SQ3R to determine who understood the major concepts. Dr. Dennison also made sure her Power Point slides listed the vocabulary terms. She always pre-taught those terms and directly related them to research methods in the course content. However, the students had to locate the vocabulary defini-tions in the textbook, along with the appropriate page numbers. She also added illustrations to the Power Points that served as a pictorial representa-tion of each term and concept. In discussion of the terms she drew them in real time with details illustrating each as a concept. As part of ongoing assessment during the semester, Dr. Dennison would ask the students to paraphrase the definition or illustration of the concept in a one minute quick write or draw.

Summary of Scenario #4

Midway through the semester, Dr. Dennison found that she needed to ensure all the readings from the textbook were online. She thought this would assist her students with their reading at home. She found that while having the readings available in this manner was helpful to some students, others did not have the financial means to activate their library accounts. Therefore, they could not take advantage of this arrangement.

She felt she had a good idea for teaching the students how to conduct an anonymous observation of human behavior. She planned to have them use their cell phone to record pictures of the behavior and post the re-sults to their Twitter accounts. However, she found that not all students had used Twitter. Dr. Dennison was surprised to find that her ideas for adjusting her course were directly related to her students' financial and experiential backgrounds.

After the course was over and Dr. Dennison had time to reflect upon her students' course evaluations, she came to several surprising conclusions about her own teaching practices. She made several insights into how her middle-upper class background and education had predisposed her to be-lieve that everyone in college had similar access and educational training. She determined that she had been naïve in thinking that all of her students had access to technology. Her biggest insight came in understanding that compliant students could complete very acceptable research work without a lot of course adjustments, but with some individual help from the instruc-tor. However, to really understand the concepts behind research methodol-ogy her students needed deeper interactions with the textbook and critical course content. She desired for her students to understand that research methodology had a structure that must be followed to be accurate and use-ful in their daily lives. Otherwise, completing a research project was simply a means to an end in completing graduate work. Her goal for the next time that she taught this class was to continue exploring instructional strategies that meet the individual needs of her students. By doing so, she hoped so that they would come to love and understand the true value of research.

APPLICATION SCENARIOS' CONCLUSIONS

After reflecting upon the above scenarios, the reader may want to reflect upon potential course adjustments. The following questions are suggested to guide that reflection process:

Questions to ask yourself:

1. What have I learned?
2. What works for my students in my setting and discipline?
3. What do I need to know, learn, or change in order to implement these changes?

The above scenarios provide only a hint of curricular, instructional, and assessment adjustments that inclusive college instructors can make to help all students learn. Adjustments such as the ones described in this book take serious thought and effort. They cannot be incorporated overnight into instructors' ways of teaching challenging course content. Individual college instructors must find individual approaches to improving their teaching and learning situations, but the general suggestions in this book can and will work in a wide variety of disciplines.

A comprehensive plan that incorporates planning, application, and then assessment of the various techniques chosen has the best hope of improving student learning and student satisfaction with the college course, its academic content, and its instructor. Even relatively easy and minor adjustments, however, can result in positive changes that benefit instructors as well as students. Making any college classroom truly inclusive is a challenging goal which will take a lifetime of dedication. Yet the rewards are so great that college instructors who sincerely wish to be inclusive will be eager to start the long journey.

AUTHORS' BIOGRAPHIES

In the Order They Appear in the Book

Moira A. Fallon, Ph.D., is an Associate Professor at the College at Brockport—State University of New York in the Department of Education and Human Development. She has conducted research in special education instructional methods for student with disabilities for more than 25 years.

Susan C. Brown, Ed.D., retired Assistant Professor of Education, has lived and worked in seven different countries. Her research interests are multicultural and global education. Her publications include *Applying Multicultural and Global Concepts in the Classroom and Beyond* (Brown & Kysilka, 2002).

Alexander B. Casareno, Ph.D., is Professor of Reading at Cosumnes River College in Sacramento, California. His teaching and research interests include the social construction of meaning in reading, learning in context, and learning within the college classroom.

Paul T. Parkison, Ed.D., is Assistant Professor of Teacher Education and Director of University Core Curriculum Assessment at the University of Southern Indiana. His primary research interests focus upon the role of teacher identity as an influential factor in the transaction between curriculum and the students' learning experiences.

Teaching Inclusively in Higher Education, pages 185–186
Copyright © 2010 by Information Age Publishing
All rights of reproduction in any form reserved.

Ellyn Lucas Arwood, Ed.D., is a speech-language pathologist and Professor in the School of Education, University of Portland, Oregon. She conducts numerous workshops and invited presentations and is the author of texts and articles on learning, language, and neuro-cognition.

Joanna Rowe Kaakinen, R.N., Ph.D., is a nurse educator and Professor in the School of Nursing, University of Portland, Oregon. She is editor of an award winning family practice nursing textbook, author of numerous articles, and a frequent presenter at conferences.

Mark Geary, Ph.D., is an Assistant Professor of Technology and Children's Literature at Dakota State University. His current research interests include using all forms of concept maps, digital video, and educational games to enhance learning.

Shelley B. Harris, Ph.D., is an Assistant Professor at Texas A&M University-San Antonio where she teaches undergraduate and graduate Reading courses. Her research interests include pre-service mentoring and induction, reflective writing, and blogging.

Jacqueline M. Ferguson, Ed.D., is an Assistant Professor at Texas A&M University -San Antonio. Prior to the position, she taught fifth grade at both Randolph-Field and Judson Independent School Districts. She still enjoys tutoring struggling readers and interacting in elementary classrooms.

Jenny C. Wilson, Ph.D., is an Assistant Professor in Reading at Texas A&M University -San Antonio. She is interested in how the world instantiates learning, how people read the world, social literacies, and how collaboration and learning go hand-in-hand.

Michelle Pulaski Behling, Ph.D., is an Assistant Professor in the Media and Communication Arts department at Pace University. Her research interests include Media Criticism, Educational Technology, and Experiential Learning.

Beth Gordon Klingner, Ph.D., is the Assistant Dean for Instructional Technology at Pace University, and is also an adjunct instructor in Media and Communication Arts and Psychology. Her research interests include Educational Technology, eLearning, Learning Styles and Social Networking.

CPSIA information can be obtained at www.ICGtesting.com
Printed in the USA
BVOW02s0203221013

334312BV00004B/47/P